Autobiography

of

John Wesley Hughes

Founder of Asbury and Kingswood College

First Fruits Press
Wilmore, Kentucky
c2013

ISBN: 9781621710295

Autobiography of John Wesley Hughes, Founder of Asbury and Kingswood College
First Fruits Press, © 2013

Digital version at
http://place.asburyseminary.edu/firstfruitsheritagematerial/18/

First Fruits Press is a digital imprint of the Asbury Theological Seminary, B.L. Fisher Library. Asbury Theological Seminary is the legal owner of the material previously published by the Pentecostal Publishing Co. and reserves the right to release new editions of this material as well as new material produced by Asbury Theological Seminary. Its publications are available for noncommercial and educational uses, such as research, teaching and private study. First Fruits Press has licensed the digital version of this work under the Creative Commons Attribution Noncommercial 3.0 United States License. To view a copy of this license, visit http://creativecommons.org/licenses/by-nc/3.0/us/.

For all other uses, contact:

First Fruits Press
B.L. Fisher Library
Asbury Theological Seminary
204 N. Lexington Ave.
Wilmore, KY 40390
http://place.asburyseminary.edu/firstfruits

Hughes, John Wesley, 1852-1932.
   Autobiography of John Wesley Hughes, founder of Asbury and Kingswood College.
   295 p., [4] leaves of plates : ill. ; 21 cm.
   Wilmore, Ky. : First Fruits Press, c2013.
   Includes a biographical chapter by Andrew Johnson and appreciations by others.
   Reprint. Previously published: Louisville, Ky. : Pentecostal Pub. Co., c1923.
   ISBN: 9781621710295 (pbk.)
   1. Hughes, John Wesley, 1852-1932. 2. Asbury College (Wilmore, Ky.) -- History. 3. Kingswood College -- History. 4. Methodist Episcopal Church, South – Kentucky -- Biography. 5. Clergy -- Kentucky -- Biography. I. Title.
BX8495 .H85 A3 2013   287.09

Cover design by Haley Hill

asburyseminary.edu
800.2ASBURY
204 North Lexington Avenue
Wilmore, Kentucky 40390

Dedication

To Mary Wallingford Hughes, The mother of Asbury aud Kingswood Colleges, and to all my old students of these two Institutions, is this Volume affectionately dedicated.

CONTENTS.

CHAPTERS.	PAGE.
Introduction	7
Foreword	11
1. Birth and Boyhood	13
2. The Man Himself	22
3. Conversion	39
4. Call to the Ministry	48
5. Educational Struggles	54
6. As a Pastor	62
7. Pastoral Work	66
8. Pastoral Work Continued	78
9. Sanctification	90
10. Origin of Asbury Clolege	99
11. Asbury's Struggles and Successes	109
12. Asbury's Conflicts and Conquests	119
13. A Trip to Palestine	128
14. Jerusalem and its Environs	148
15. Homeward Bound	158
16. Kingswood College	168
17. As a Theological Teacher	178
18. As a College President	196
19. Holiness Camp Meetings	215
20. Mary Wallingford Hughes	222
21. Greater Asbury	229
22. As a Preacher	235
23. Appreciations	247

INTRODUCTION.

BY DR. H. C. MORRISON.

At the solicitation of many friends, Rev. John Wesley Hughes, D.D., has consented to write an autobiographical sketch of his life. It will only be a sketch. A man who has lived as many years and has been as constantly in active service as John Wesley Hughes has been will not be able to put his life into a book,—no, not into several large volumes.

Doctor Hughes was converted at the age of sixteen. God gave him a most gracious experience of salvation. He answered his call to the ministry with enthusiasm and zeal and for many years he has been a most faithful minister of the Gospel. Brother Hughes was especially gifted with evangelistic fervor and was one of the leaders in bringing into the Kentucky Conference the old-time Methodist revivals which had, for a number of years, been sadly neglected.

The Blue Grass Region of Kentucky had keenly felt the blight of Campbellism which had ridiculed the mourner's bench, the regeneration and witnessing power of the Holy Ghost, and unfortnately, in many Methodist churches people were asked to join the church without being invited to the altar of prayer, without insistence that they must be born again before they were proper subjects for membership in the church of the Lord Jesus Christ.

INTRODUCTION

Hughes lifted aloft the banner of true Methodism, drew the sword of the Spirit and with a holy daring, championed the cause of true repentance, the new birth, and the clear witness of the Holy Ghost to a conscious salvation. God wonderfully blessed his ministry. He not only held great revivals in his own charges, but was called from place to place by his brother-pastors and under his ministry God kindled many powerful revivals of true religion.

He had so many calls from his brother-ministers, the need was so great, and his soul was so deeply interested in the salvation of sinners and the sanctification of believers that he gave up the regular pastorate and for a time devoted himself entirely to evangelistic work. He was a devoted lover of young people and deeply interested in their spiritual progress and life service after being saved in his meetings. He directed many of his converts to various schools and was alarmed to find that not a few of them backslid and that frequently the teachings in the schools were entirely different from those he had given from the pulpit and at the altar of prayer. It was because of these conditions that he determined to found a college where students might not only be well educated, but their spiritual life well developed.

Searching for a place suitable for the purpose he had in mind, Doctor Hughes visited Wilmore, Kentucky, and selected this beautiful center of the Blue Grass region of Kentucky and made it the home of Asbury College. The school was founded at the time when a bitter battle of opposition and persecution was being conducted against the Methodist people who professed the experience of entire sanctification. The new enterprise called for genuine faith in God and great personal courage. These were two of Doctor Hughes' most outstanding qualities.

Throughout the fifteen years that he was president and owner of Asbury College he occupied the chair of theology and philosophy. He was a steadfast believer in the Word of God. He had implicit faith in the atonement wrought out upon the cross by Jesus Christ, and fully recognized the personality and presence of the Holy Ghost.

The sacrifices he made and the intense labor he put into these years of service at Asbury have been amply rewarded by the successful and fruitful service of pastors, evangelists, misionaries and teachers who have gone out into the world winning great multitudes of souls to our Saviour. His students believed in him. They loved him and they took delight in talking together over the intense earnestness with which he *pounded* the old Methodist doctrines into them. His prayers have followed them and now that he is facing toward the evening of life he looks out with joy over the great harvest field in which those educated under his care and direction are laboring for Christ and humanity. As the evening draws on apace, his soul is mellow with love; he holds with strengthening grip the great doctrines of the Bible expounded and proclaimed by the father and founder of the Methodist Church, finding sweet comfort and peace in the fullness of salvation and the assurance of blessed immortality.

His love for Asbury College abides and he watches the growth and progress of the school with intense interest and a jealous desire that it may never depart in doctrine, experience or practice from its original purpose and aim. This autobiography will be read with intense interest and profit. It is a contribution, in its way, to Methodism,—wider still, to experimental Christianity. It is full of the spirit of the Gospel. It will prove a religious tonic of interest and quickening to all who read its pages.

Brother Hughes is a strong, active man today with much good service in him. May the Lord grant that the evening of his life be extended; that his sun go down slowly, and no doubt on the other shore he will meet with multitudes who have been led to Christ through his faithful and zealous ministry.

FOREWORD.

This book is an answer to the many requests which for years have come from my old students, teachers and friends, urging me to write a story of my life and the history of Asbury and Kingswood Colleges.

(1) My first objective in penning the present volume is in keeping with the one great primary purpose of my Christian life—the glorification of God, the evangelization of the world, the conversion of sinners, the sanctification of believers, the instruction of Christians and the edification of saints.

(2) To preserve in permanent form a true, authentic history of Asbury and Kingswood Colleges; to give a correct official record of their origin, progress, work and development under my administration.

(3) In giving the story of my life, my education by experience in the "University of Hard Knocks" I hope to stimulate and to encourage the youth of the land, the rising generation to their respective callings, and to fully prepare themselves for faithful and efficient service in the field of Christian activity.

(4) To preach, by means of the printed page, to more people while I live and after I am gone.

(5) To create what is to be known as the *Hughes Ministerial Memorial Loan Fund* to aid

worthy young men and women in Asbury College to prepare for life's work. The money used for this purpose is to be paid back and reinvested.

(6) To acknowledge my profound gratitude and obligations to my old student, Rev. Andrew Johnson, D.D., for the splendid chapters he has contributed to the book. I do not believe that any school in this country has sent out a more gifted thinker, writer, platform speaker and preacher than Dr. Johnson.

The splendid *Appreciations* given in this Volume by many of my old students and teachers, practically representing the student body and faculty, mean more to me than wealth, reputation or monuments in marble or stone.

This book possibly would not have been written but for the urgency and hearty co-operation of Sadie P. Hughes, my wife.

J. W. HUGHES.

CHAPTER I.

BIRTH AND BOYHOOD.

On the sixteenth day of May, 1852, I was born in Owen County, Northwestern Kentucky. I know but little of my ancestors. My father was born in Culpepper County, Virginia, known in those days as the Old Dominion. I was told by my mother that my father was brought to what was then known the Kentucky County by his parents in one of the then usual ways, namely: Large home-made baskets and the parents rode horse-back and the children rode in the baskets thrown across the horses, being no roads or highways in those days. I visited Culpepper County some time ago and had a research lady help me look up some of my ancestors. I told her this story, feeling a little abashed because of the poverty of my parents. But she read me a number of records where some of the best families of that country traveled in similar ways. My mother also told me that my father came to the west with his parents when Lexington, Kentucky was a mere village of about a half a dozen houses, (now about forty thousand inhabitants) but his parents went on past this ideal country as it now is, of course then a wilderness, to the hill country and located in what is known as the waters of Eagle Creek, which bordered my father's farm. My father died sixty-eight years ago when I was too young to have any recollection of him. I have been informed by those who knew him that he was a typical Kentucky gentleman of the middle class of wealth and reputation for his day. I have also been told that I reminded them more of him than any of his children, for he had two families of children, my mother being his second wife.

My widowed mother was left with a hundred acres of hill land and plain log buildings as a home in which to rear her children. Her former name was Anna Eliza Guill, belonging to one of the substantial families of that day. Her grandfather fought three years in the Revolutionary War. Being left an orphan she was well acquainted with the difficulties of taking care of herself before her marriage; and after marriage of her children with but little of this world's goods. She was an unconverted member of the Methodist Church, and not therefore capable of leading her children to God by precept and example, which I profoundly regret, but was known to be absolutely honest, paying her just debts, and teaching her children to make their word their bond and to live a moral, upright life and I have never known the day when I retired at night that I **had** not honestly tried to keep the teachings of my mother. She also taught the dangers of immorality on all lines, and particularly on the lines of liquor, which was used in those days by the average family as they use the different kinds of wines in Europe, very similar to the way we use milk and coffee.

At the age of sixteen I discovered I had an appetite for strong drink and became somewhat intoxicated twice and made a vow that never again should a drop of intoxicants enter my mouth and I have kept that vow to this day.

In those old-fashioned days most everybody wore home-made clothing including their footwear. Many children went barefooted part or all of the winter. I very distinctly recall a bit of sarcasm that a neighbor boy got off on my brother Nathan (now a doctor in Waverly, Illinois) and myself, when we got our brass-toed and red-topped boots as Christmas gifts. (In those days Christmas gifts were almost unknown.) He had gotten his boots weeks before and had worn the new off of them. He came over and saw brother and myself with our new ones which to me, as I saw it then, was the finest footwear I have ever seen or worn. He looked at our new boots, then glanced at his own and said, "Boys, the only thing I have to say is that you did not get them before you needed them." My readers will recall the fact that in those early days we did not know anything about modern clothing, modes of living, modes of travel, modes of cooking, railroads and telephones and telegraph lines as we do in these modern times. I was a young man when I saw my first cooking stove, but "dear me" I shall never forget the splendid cooking of my dear old country mother. We would build a big fire in a large chimney where we might with comfort in the coldest winter evenings sit in the middle of the house. Mother would bring in a long-handled skillet and lid, put them on the fire and later put them down on the beds of red-hot coals, roll out her corndodgers, or sometimes wheat bread, stroking her knife over it both ways, putting coals of fire on the lid; then she hung the spare rib on a hook suspended from the chimney and roasted it, took out the hot dodgers or wheat bread, and roasted rib, and with plenty of rich milk and country butter we had such a meal, if I am to trust my childhood memory, as I have never sat down to since. It makes my mouth "water" to think of it this late day. Oh, to go back to the simplicity of my childhood is worth while in my mature days. You will say, "You are a little antiquated." This I admit, but I shall never regret that I had the good fortune to be born and reared poor and honest. First, because the Child born in the manger two thousand years ago, lived a faultless life among men thirty-three years, was so poor in this world's goods, that he said, "Foxes have holes and the birds of the air have nests; but the Son of man hath not where to lay his head."

I assume, therefore, that poverty is not a disgrace and never has been.

Second. Because all history shows that the masses of people have been born, lived and died, at least in comparative poverty. All will recall the saying of Abraham Lincoln, taken out of his own experience, "God must have loved poor people or he would not have made so many of them."

Third. Because the boy or girl who is born with but little of this world's goods, having to make his own living from his childhood as did his parents,

BIRTH AND BOYHOOD

knows the value of a dollar and the real value of making his living by the sweat of his brow. I am heartily sorry for a rich man's son. From the fact that he often is dependent upon his parents for his support and life's equipment which is liable to make him helpless when the parent's aid is withdrawn. As an illustration, during the years of slavery in the South the sons of slave-holders really were more injured or cursed by slavery than were the slaves themselves. When the Emancipation Proclamation was made, the major part of these sons were helpless, having been often brought up in luxury and idleness and of course dependent and, sad to say, in many cases in consequence of their idleness, yielded to the curse of amalgamation of the races. It was a common fad in those ante-bellum days among the whites and colored to call the non-slave holders of the South "Poor white trash." Of course this produced two distinct classes, and more or less bitterness in consequence. God and all right-thinking people know that poverty or moderate means of this world's goods contrasted with wealth does not make one class the nobility and the other class the ignoble. Now as never before man is estimated by popular sentiment not for his ancestral blood, wealth or social standing, but for his own intrinsic worth in serving his God and his fellow man. If, therefore, I have been of any value to the world it has not been because of nobility of blood or of wealth.

I was considered a vivacious and rollicsome boy, always occupied in some way when not asleep. I soon discovered that life was a race and that I had to run or get run over. So I made up my mind to run. If I got in a crowd of associates I aimed to act my part in the best way possible whether in work or in fun. If I got in a crowd of gleeful, fun-making boys I acted my part; if nothing was going on, I started something. I never saw a boy do a thing in the water or out of it that I did not try to do it a little better than he did. I felt if it was worth doing at all, it was worth doing well. I always came out ahead if possible. I was a natural mimic of all the animals I ever saw. When I came in contact with them I either drew them to me by making similar calls to their own, or else dispersed them in fear. I never aimed to do anything to injure anybody or anything, but played many pranks on my fellows and sometimes on the lower animals. One Sunday in returning home at noon from a day of desecration in the creek and elsewhere, finding, as I thought nobody at home I went to the cupboard, got my dinner, and feeling a little lonely I concluded to have a cat fight. I tied a couple of cats by their caudal appendages, threw them over a clothes line and had a decided civil war for a few moments, at which time their tails became separated and each one, as far as I could see, fled for the north or south pole. I enjoyed it immensely. Soon I heard a hideous noise, and having some conscience qualm of my treatment of these animals, I thought God had sent the devil after me. It scared me almost to death. I left the house as rapidly as my pedestrian extremities would take me up the hill, hid behind the fence and looked back to see if I could see any interpretation of that noise. My sisters who had secluded themselves and had made this noise, came out to see what had become of me. My nerves were reduced to normal tension when I saw it was not the devil.

On another occasion, some boys and myself were fighting bumble bees, having stirred up their nests. This was great fun for us boys. My brother Nathan refused to join us. I dared him and said, "If you were not a coward you would help us fight them." He then joined us and was stung on the upper lip. In a minute his lip was so swollen that he could scarcely talk. He never swore an oath but had one word that was indicative of his wrath and hearty indignation. He said, "Dag-on-you, I told you what would happen if I went into it.' We had some real, old-fashioned boy fun!

I want to say to the boys and girls who read these little stories of my boyhood days that I seldom practiced a prank on my fellows when it was displeasing or hurtful to them, and only tell these stories to show you that I was a real boy.

The first time I discovered that I might make a real man, a gentleman and lady on horseback rode by my brother and myself where we were cutting weeds on our mother's farm. He did not speak but his wife said, "Howdy do, little boys. I am sure you are industrious and will make good men." I then began to discover that I had aspiration and wanted to be of service to my fellowman.

I do not know how far back I began to think seriously of God and religion and I feel sure if I had had the right instruction I would have given my heart to God when a child. I always reverenced the church, the ministry, and godly people, and particularly old people.

When I became a Christian and saw and felt most keenly the absolute need of a collge education I began to discover myself. I do not believe that anything on intellectual, spiritual and religious lines can come into the human life so inspirational as a clear case of Bible salvation. In those crucial moments as I emerged into manhood with the all absorbing desire for a real education I made up my mind to have it at any cost. Of course having no early training on educational lines in common with most of my associates I had to go to the bottom for the rudiments of an education. I shall never be able to tell understandingly to those who have not had similar experiences the torture and mortification of being classified with children five and six years of age in learning how to spell, read and write and securing other rudimentary branches of education. I am absolutely certain if I had not had the grace of God in my soul I would have fainted and fallen by the way. But so soon as God saved my soul at the age of sixteen, I was called of Him not only to make the most of myself, but to preach the everlasting Gospel. So soon as I could get a sufficient education (by working awhile and going to school awhile) to teach public school I had an insatiable hunger for

BIRTH AND BOYHOOD

a college education. I was the first person ever to go away from our community in order to secure a college education. I began the study and practice of economics when quite a youth. My half brother, a moneyed man for those days, said to me, "John, take care of the cents and the dollars will take care of themselves." That has been my life motto. I am sure I am correct in saying that when I was twenty-five years old I had not spent five dollars foolishly.

My first business enterprise was dropping corn at twenty-five cents a day. My second—I secured a pig that belonged to a large litter that failed to get its quota of rashings, and in consequence was regarded as worthless. I took it home, gave it a genteel bath, plenty of food and it grew rapidly and became a mother and I disposed of the lot for money enough to buy my first store suit, shoes, hat, white shirt, necktie with two silver strips down the center of it, which I shall never forget. My third enterprise, I cleared a piece of land at odd times, when not busy on the farm, for the corn I could raise on it in two years. With this I bought my first saddle, bridle and blanket. And when the crops were laid by on my mother's farm I worked four months for a two-year-old colt. One Sunday morning, a little after sun-up, I groomed my colt and myself with our new outfit and went to church where the pulpit was between the doors and had the opportunity to show my new suit, which I felt sure everybody was viewing closely, and have never felt my importance so much from that day to this.

CHAPTER II.

THE MAN HIMSELF.

The history of the world is the biography of great men. In all the events and activities recounted in the Annals of Time the human and personal element has played the most prominent and conspicuous role. Abstract ideas, views, laws, principles, yea, things, facts and phenomena all have their source and center in man the crown of creation. The estimation of man's merit and moral worth has released floods of oratory and sent volumes afloat on the tides of literary lore.

The Psalmist of old asks the question—"What is man that thou art mindful of him?" Democratus, one of the early Greek philosophers, declared that man is the measure of the universe. Shakespeare, the myriad-minded, commented on the majesty of man in these memorable words—

"What a noble piece of work is man,
In moving and address, how admirable!
In apprehension, how like an angel!
In understanding how like a God!
The companion of saints the paragon of animals."
Sir William Hamilton, than whom no greater philosopher ever lived said: "There is nothing great in the Universe but man, and nothing great in man but mind." Bob Burns, *mali exempli*, who nevertheless made classic the tongue of the Scotchmen and

rooted himself in the affections of the English-speaking world, magnified the manhood of man in the immortal poem—"A man's a man, for a'that and a'that."

It is true that man is known and estimated by his works, characterized by calling and career. As a rule he is viewed and reviewed in his relationship to others. President Hyde, in his "Five Great Philosophies of Life," says:—"Strip a man of his relations and you have no man left. The man who is neither son, brother, husband, father, citizen, neighbor, or workman is inconceivable." While this is true, yet we recognize the fact that prior to and back of all musical creations, poetic productions, literary works, military achievements, scientific inventions, modern discoveries, mechanical appliances, industrial accomplishments, commercial activities and institutional establishments stands man, the master of all his works and the monarch of all he surveys. Let us, then, as far as possible, forget for the time being the office, the function, the occupation, the position, the calling, and the career and direct our attention to the man himself. In order to appreciate the power, personality, disposition and characteristic traits of Dr. J. W. Hughes, the subject of our sketch, it is necessary to take into the biological account, three things—*heredity, environment* and the *grace of God*. We all receive some sort of heritage from the past. The racial instinct, the national dynamic of blood, the ancestral tribe, the family tree, the parent stock and stamina all have more or less to do in our moulding and making. We have examined the biographical records of the Hughes family in the United States and find a number of prominnet educators, legislators and military celebrities.

Dr. Hughes' grandfather was one of the early settlers in Owen County, having moved with his family from Culpepper County, Virginia, after the Revolutionary War. It cuts no figure with him that he failed to inherit fame and fortune from his forebears. He stands on his own merit, and takes no stock in tracing genealogies through a long list of illustrious ancestral celebrities. He congratulates himself and counts it a blessing that he was not born with a "silver spoon in his mouth" and cradled in the lazy lap of luxury. He esteems it a greater honor to have come from humble parentage than to have descended in pomp and pageantry from the titled ranks of distinguished nobility. Nevertheless he came from the greatest race in the world—the Caucasian race; from the greatest stock of that race, the Anglo-Saxon stock; from the best class of citizens in the country, the middle class, the great American commonality; running through his veins is the pure blood of honorable Virginia parentage, while he himself was born and bred in old Kentucky. This constitutes a great genealogical background for any boy and gives him a patent and passport of self-respect with his fellow countrymen.

Following the formative forces of heredity, comes the question of Nature's environment. We cannot escape the fact that the life of an individual is affected by its surroundings and tinctured with the times of which it is a representative. Environmental influence, meant much to Dr. Hughes' early life. It was his good fortune to have been born and brought up on the farm, far removed from the sights and scenes and sins of city life. He breathed the pure air of God's great outdoors, romped and played in the green meadows, chased the golden-winged butterfly, watched the eagle in its wild flight, climbed the crumbling cliffs and velvet slopes of the hoary hills of sweet Owen county. He wandered in the wild-wood under the green roof of trees, heard the call of the squirrel and the flutter of the bird and the music of the rippling rill and the murmuring brook.

As a farmer boy he enjoyed a great variety of sports such as fishing, swimming, trapping, hunting, playing ball, bull-pen, round town, marbles and many other exercises and activities. This rough and tumble out-door life is the favorite method that Nature employs to build brain and brawn. John's work as a farmer lad on the hills and in the valleys of sweet Owen comprised quite an industrial program. He ran errands and did chores—cut wood, built fires, rolled logs, piled rocks, plowed corn, hoed potatoes, pulled weeds, fed chickens, "slopped" the pigs, drove the cows, fed the horses, mowed grass, mauled rails, sawed timber, harvested wheat and gathered in the grain. A lot of the frontier farmer work, such as log-rolling, house-raising, wheat threshing and hog-killing was not dull drudgery but a delight to the eager and energetic country boy.

With such a bill of fare in the fine and flowing fields of the agricultural world, no wonder statistics tell us that ninety-five percent of the great men of our nation came off the farm. If we trace the footsteps of John Hughes across the furrowed fields and up the rugged hills of rustic life we may more fully understand how these early days of diversified industry built into his belligerent constitution the vim and vigor, iron and oak of an indomitable disposition, and laid the foundation for that indefatigable zeal for which he has always been noted. It took a strong man, seasoned for war and armed for conflict and not a little diletante dude, plumed and perfumed and fitted out with all the delicate finery and femininity, to tackle and triumph over the hard problems that confronted John W. Hughes in his educational struggles, ministerial life and college career.

A boy must have mental, moral and muscular development in order to make a full-orbed man. The opportunities and advantages of a literary education, moral and religious training are pre-eminently important and paramount in the moulding and making of a human life. Fortune did not favor the boy, John Hughes, during the days of his early childhood, on educational and religious lines. He tells us elsewhere in this Volume, that he was sixteen years of age before he could read or write. He was conspicuous for his absence in the old log-cabin school house famous in the memoirs of so many American men. He was kept busy at home working hard to help support his widowed mother. The boy whose schooling is extremely limited or wholly neglected in the plastic days of impressionable youth will have to pay up and make up for lost time. This is exactly what John Hughes did when once the alarm bell was rung in the dormitory of his soul and he woke up to realize his need of an education. It looks like a very late start on literary lines for a boy sixteen years of age and unable to read or write. But it must be remembered that the educational advantages were very meager in many communties in the rural districts of Kentucky fifty years ago. John Hughes was not lonesome in his literary limitations and lack of learning, for he dwelt in the midst of a people of uneducated lips. In fact he was the first boy in all the region round about to go off to college. A genuine, old-time, clear-cut, sky-blue conversion marked the great turning point in his life. It completely revolutionized him on all lines. He began to study in earnest and soon caught up with the procession and qualified himself as a country schoolteacher and later attended college and Vanderbilt University.

We have seen how his early out-door life was set and surrounded with high hills, picturesquec valleys, sparkling streams, shady woods, blooming flowers, and sapphire skies. Let us now turn our eyes from these rustic scenes of the rural districts of sweet Owen county and direct our attention to the personal appearance and physical constitution of the subject of our sketch—the man himself. When we hear a great deal of the name and fame of any particular person we have a curiosity to know what he looks like. There are three ways of satisfying this common curiosity of mankind—a personal view, to see him for ourselves; a photographic view, to see his picture, and a biographical view, or a pen picture of his personal appearance. The old students of Asbury and thousands who have seen and known Dr. Hughes personally do not need any pen picture. They remember him well. His photo only gives a faint view. We are not artistic and can give but a rough outline of his physical form and personal appearance. Dr. Hughes is built on the order of Andrew Jackson and Abraham Lincoln. He is tall, lean, athletic, with the natural lines of leadership. He walks with a high swinging step as though he is going somewhere. He has curly auburn hair, almost red (now silvered over with the snows of many winters. Yet there is no snow on his heart,) small blue, expressive eyes; thin, clean-cut lips that tell of tremendous determination. The general cast of his countenance is a combination of firmness, frankness and kindness. His features are well-formed and regular, yet he is not as handsome as a Grecian Apollo or a Roman Adonis. He is not a pampered product of the parlor, but a product of the farm, rugged and masculine, the tall sycamore of Owen. The quick emphatic swing of his right arm when in sermonic action defies all the movements of Delsarte gesticulations. The boys in college used to say that his coat-tails cracked like a waggoner's whip. When expounding some great truth his voice often sounded like the explosive peals of imperative thunder. He is firm and unshaken in his convictions. He was never at any time found on both sides of the same question. "Absolutely and unequivocally" was one of his favorite expressions. His former students doubtless remember how he could use these double adverbs with such a positive ring of certainty as to expel the last lingering doubt on any proposition to which he applied them. "A thousand times no!" was one of his favorite forms of emphasizing the negative. It was not necessary to ask his position the second time on questions answerable by yes or no. He did not mince words or evade issues. He has a mind that grasps truth clearly and clings to it tenaciously. Beyond a peradventure he is one of the best posted men in this country on the fundamental doctrines of Christianity.

In his social disposition and general make-up he is undoubtedly and redeemedly democratic. While he is absolutely uncompromising on principles, he is one of the most affable and approachable of all men. All classes can come into his presence with perfect ease. He never tried to put on any bull-dog aristocracy. He has the courage and the capacity to converse with great men and the democratic condescension to make the most humble and illiterate feel free in his presence.

No characterization of an individual is complete that omits the question of temperament. The different kinds of temperament have been classified as follows—sanguine, nervous, billious, phlegmatic and tempered temperament. It is very difficult to classify some people temperamentally. They cut counter and cross and are mixed and complicated. It is hard to place them on any proposition. But not so with John W. Hughes. He is clear-cut, pronounced, out-and-out, full-fledged and four-square. In his constitutional make-up he is manifestly of the nervous temperament. But the nervous temperament is not synonymous with nervousness. Dr. Hughes is like the Apostle Peter, active, energetic, alert, impulsive and impetuous. God entrusted in his hand the key that opened the door into the collegiate world of holiness institutions.

It took a man of indefatigable zeal, irrepressible enthusiasm, indomitable will and extraordinary energy to accomplish the herculean task of founding and establishing an institution like Asbury College. He was a whole galvanic battery of concentrated energy and spiritual enthusiasm within himself. Back in his palmy days it seemed that he could stir, stimulate, inspire and pump more enthusiasm into college pupils than any man living. If we were to select one chief characteristic in the constitutional make-up of a human life, as when we say that Abraham is noted for faith, Moses for meekness, Joshua for courage, Job for patience, Daniel for boldness, Joseph for purity, Peter for impetuosity, James for practicality—or when we characterize Amos as the prophet of morality, Hosea as the prophet of love, Ezekiel as the prophet of individualism, Jeremiah as the prophet of personal piety, Isaiah as the prophet of universalism, Matthew as the evangelist of the Kingdom, Mark as the evangelist of service, Luke as the evangelist of humanity and John as the evangelist of Deity—we would say that John W. Hughes is noted for energy. While a person may be noted, he cannot be known by one single prominent feature in his character or career. In order to get anything like a fair, full view of one's life we must widen the lens in the field-glass of historical investigation and sweep the whole domain of human endeavor.

Dr. Hughes not only possesses power, energy, enthusiasm and impetuosity but common sense and sound judgment. There may be enthusiasm without judgment and judgment without enthusiasm. But with the founder of Asbury College there was a combination of the two elements—enthusiasm plus judgment. Down through the vicissitudes and meandering scenes of his life many instances of the exercise of good judgment may be pointed out. Far-sighted sagacity and sound judgment are seen in his selection of the location of Asbury College. He picked out a fine spot in the famous Blue Grass regions of old Kentucky. He showed splendid judgment when he selected a college curriculum for Asbury. He placed education and religion on that high plane of perfect reciprocity. He did not advocate religion at the expense of education; and he did not advance education at the sacrifice of religion. He wisely emphasized not only religion but full salvation without neglecting education. He successfully demonstrated to the world that the education of the heart and head, in the highest sense of the term, could be carried on in one common collegiate course. He also exercised the finest kind of judgment in steering the bark of his newly-founded educational institution clear of the Charybdis of formalism on the one hand and the Scylla of fanaticism on the other. He kept the college straight on the great fundamental principles and cardinal doctrines of Christianity. In all his long college and ministerial career he was never once known to fight the church as an organized institution. "You always kept the college in contact with the church," said one of the leading bishops of the Southern Methodist Church in congratulating Dr. Hughes for his constructive management of the institution.

Again and again Dr. Hughes' good judgment crops out. It is seen in his wise selection of a wife. When he was a young minister on a pastoral charge he exercised a first-class judgment in the selection of a most suitable wife. Mrs. Mary W. Hughes, the memorable mother of Asbury College, to whom a glowing tribute is devoted in one of the chapters of this volume, was an ideal helpmeet and companion for many years of a well-mated, happy married life. Several years after she passed to her eternal reward, Dr. Hughes felt free to choose another companion. In his second marriage he exercised the same good judgment in the selection of a most suitable companion. Many a man fails in the selection of a second wife. But Dr. Hughes' judgment was unerring in this regard.

THE MAN HIMSELF

Dr. Hughes has always been noted for his courage and holy boldness. When the great polemical conflict was raging on the fields of full salvation, he stood like a Stonewall Jackson and faced every foe. He had the courage of a Martin Luther when it came to the defense of the doctrine of Bible holiness. He would testify to the experience of entire sanctification at annual conferences in the presence of bishops, secretaries and all kinds of dignitaries.

At all times and under all circumstances, he has stood as firm as the Rock of Gibraltar on this great gospel truth. On one occasion he visited the temple of John Alexander Dowie in Chicago. Dowie, as everybody knows, was a regular Goliath of Gath in brandishing his sword, bluffing his way and bantering the world. He could brow-beat the crowd and intimidate the average person when he rolled up his sleeves, rattled his armor, shook his long robes and sallied forth upon the sons of Sceva. But he met his match when he ran up against the bosses of Hughes' buckler. It was a battle of Johns, John Hughes vs. John Dowie. Newspaper men had flung ink at Dowie from a distance. Preachers had answered his pretensions from their own pulpits far away. But the indomitable John Hughes bearded the lion in his den. He went to see Dowie and discussed religious views face to face. During his visit he went into Dowie's temple to hear him preach. In his bombastic discourse Dowie began a tirade against the Methodist preachers for baptizing babies. "It is a damnable heresy," he shouted. "If it is not (pointing in the direction of Dr. Hughes) deny it you Kentucky Methodist preachers if you dare." He hurled this challenge with all the pomposity, audacity and bombasity that he could command. With a strong, quick, powerful and imperative voice, Dr. Hughes shouted back, like a clap of thunder from a clear sky—No!! A volley of no's followed from the crowd. Dowie surprised and discomfited, jumped and whirled around on the platform, slapped his hands on his chest as though he had received a pugilistic knock-out blow, crestfallen and confused, he continued his sermon without making any further reply.

One of the most noble traits that was ever narrated in the life of a real red-blooded man is the inestimable prize of social purity. While many ministers have been wrecked on the rock of social impurity, Dr. Hughes has a moral record above reproach and disrepute. There has never been one single blot upon his social escutcheon, either before or after his conversion. In the midst of a world of temptation he has lived a social life pure as the lily.

A man's greatness is measured by the touchstone of tender sympathies. He may have prestige, fame, nobility, honor, riches, wit, wisdom, knowledge and eloquence, but if he has not the soul of sympathy, he is become a "sounding brass or tinkling cymbal." Dwight L. Moody, the world-famed evangelist, who founded the Northfield Institutions of learning was commended far and near because he took his students into his College and Seminary at half-rates.

But with greater mercy and magnanimity Dr. Hughes threw wide open the doors of Asbury College to many students who were not able to pay any tuition at all. During his presidency of the Institution he was never known to turn a student away for the lack of tuition. This act is almost unparalleled in the history of human events and deserves to be written in letters of gold upon the imperishable monuments of mankind.

Someone has said that an honest man is the noblest work of God. In a world of greed and graft, rascality and dishonesty it is a lasting benediction and a veritable vindication of honor and integrity to be able to point to a man who is known for the honesty of his dealings with his fellowmen. Dr. Hughes has handled in his day and for his day a considerable sum of money. He gained and held the confidence of big business men and bankers. He was able to walk up to a bank and borrow any amount at any time.

As a man, minister and college president he practiced and inculcated economy. He was a regular Thomas Jefferson in the economical administration of all his affairs. While he dressed decently, he never tried to doll up or act the dude or play the role of a Chesterfield in bull-dog dignity, pomp and pageantry. He was and is a man's man—a man among men. Ruskin declared that the first great test of a truly great man is his humility. We all have our strong points, our weak points, our peculiar points and our points in common. The historian is supposed to emphasize the characteristic features, the strong and peculiar points in the subject of his biographical sketch. The Bible is about the only book in the whole world that lays bare the defects and weak points of a person's life. It is customary to sum up or to group the main characteristic points of the person represented in a biographical production. For instance Dr. A. T. Pearson, the noted author, gives the following summary of the life of George Mueller, founder of the Bristol Orphanage:

1. Conversion.
2. Missionary Spirit.
3. Renunciation of Self.
4. Taking counsel of God.
5. Humble and childlike temper.
6. Plain method of preaching.
7. Cutting loose from man or human dependence.
8. Satisfaction in the Word of God.
9. Thorough Bible Study.
10. Freedom from human control.
11. Use of opportunity.
12. Release from civil obligations.
13. Waiting on God for message.
14. Submission to the authority of the Word.
15. Voluntary offerings—liberal in giving.
16. Surrender of all earthly possessions.
17. Habit of secret prayer.
18. Jealousy of his testimony.
19. Organizing of his work—systematic.
20. Sympathy with orphans.

THE MAN HIMSELF

This brief outline gives one a glimpse into the personal life of that great man Mueller, who was known the world over for his mighty faith in God.

A certain biographer gives the following summary of Dwight L. Moody's personal traits and chief characteristics:—
1. Great natural endowments.
2. Self sacrifice.
3. Wisdom profounder than that of schools.
4. Self-confidence (initiative).
5. Great moral courage.
6. Exhaustless stock of common sense.
7. Simplicity.
8. Knowledge of Bible.
9. Rare master of men.
10. Plain matter-of-fact man.
11. Love and tenderness.
12. Surcharged with magnetism.

This certainly gives a very succinct and concise description of that world-famed and phenominally successful evangelist.

We are not comparing Dr. Hughes to Moody or Mueller. Yet we had rather have the honor of founding Asbury College than the honor of founding the Bristol Orphanage, or the Northfield Institutions. Let us sum up the personal traits and chief characteristics of Dr. Hughes.
1. Definite, positive, pronounced.
2. Extraordinary amount of energy.
3. Thoroughness in method and work.
4. Common sense and sound judgment.

5. Courage and holy boldness.
6. Persistence and tremendous tenacity.
7. Democratic spirit—principle—no partisan spirit.
8. Sympathetic toward the struggling student.
9. Prudence in all social relationship.
10. Economical in personal or public expense.
11. Great efficiency as theological teacher.
12. Unequivocal—uncompromising in principle.
13. Zealous and enthusiastic.
14. Firm and emphatic on fundamentals.

These fourteen points or features, as discussed in this chapter, furnish a kind of index, a second introduction, as it were, to the man, the narration and description of whose life and labors, both biographical and autobiographical are to fill the pages of the present volume. When a man distinguishes himself on any certain line, when he rises superior to his fellowmen in any particular field of activity, when he does common things uncommonly well; when his life is an inspiration and well worthy of imitation; when he is a benediction and a great benefactor to mankind; when he has founded a famous institution for the furtherance of a worthy cause he is entitled to a place on the pages of biographical history. The founding of such an institution as Asbury College is sufficient to immortalize any man. This one fact alone even, if there were nothing else to his credit, entitles Dr. John W. Hughes to an honorable place among the biographies of the world.

ANDREW JOHNSON.

CHAPTER III.

CONVERSION.

There cannot be too much said about home environment where children are to be born and reared. It is a fearful responsibility to become a parent and to be the cause of immortal souls coming into the world, which means a curse or a blessing to the cause of God and mankind. No child can be well bred and born, in a religious sense, in a home that ignores God. No blue blood, culture, or wealth can be substituted for a godly home. I was not reared in a religious home, it grieves my heart to say.

I am sure that I was almost always under conviction for sin from the time I was twelve years old. Until I entered my seventeenth year, I did not know what was the matter with me as I had not been taught the meaning of conviction. I joined the church in a mere protracted meeting with fifty-six other converts. I am sure, there was not a single one that was born of the Spirit. I was an honest, sincere seeker after God and real salvation. I availed myself of all the light I could get from preachers and people, but failed to get to Christ—a sad thing to occur in a soul anxious to get to God. God pity the preacher or church, that does not know how to lead sinners to Christ! The following questions were asked me in common with other converts:

"Do you feel yourself a sinner?" I answered, "I do."

"Do you feel sorry for your sins and want to forsake them?" I answered, "I do."

"Do you love God?" As an uninstructed sinner, I answered, "I hope so."

"Do you love the church and desire to become a member of it?" I answered, "I do." For I was a stranger in the community and had no difficulty with anyone in or out of the church at that place. Of course I knew nothing of the significance of the real Church of God, neither knowing God nor the import of the question, for the doctrines of repentance toward God, faith in our Lord Jesus Christ, the new birth and witness of the Holy Spirit had not been emphasized, which are absolutely essential for the salvation of a lost soul.

The preacher then said, "All in favor of receiving this young man into the church raise your right hand." Their hands went up and their heads went down, for I watched them. I never shall forget the impression it made on my young heart, as I looked into the *forlorn* and *joyless faces* of that congregation. I said in my sad and hungry heart, "If this is all there is in religion, I wish I had not started;" and have the same opinion to this day, after fifty-four years of experience and observation, for a Christian experience is the biggest thing a human soul ever sought and obtained in this world. I am absolutely certain, after a trial of a half century, it excels all other earthly possessions. My disappointed, restless heart hoped when I was baptized in water I would find soul-rest, but my hungry heart was still doomed to disappointment. After I was taken down to the creek and immersed, for my church and baptismal vows obligated me to separate myself from all worldly practices, customs, and enjoyments, and gave me nothing in their stead that was satisfying to my soul, I wished, from the bottom of my heart, that I had not joined the church.

In this confused and restless condition, I felt I was neither prepared to live nor die; and when the total eclipse of the sun came I was scared out of my wits, for I was afraid that the Judgment Day had come, and I would have to meet God unprepared. I knew nothing at all about the sun's eclipse; and my fears were relieved when the sun again showed his cheery face.

During the Christmas holidays, I visited my home from which I had been absent several months. I had planned to spend the Christmas holidays with my old neighbor boys and girls and associates, hunting in the day and going to socials at night. A wonderful, old-fashioned revival of religion had been going on for many weeks, sweeping like a prairie fire over the neighborhood, extending for miles in different directions bringing hundreds of souls to God in that time and its onward sweep in the coming weeks.

As far back as I could remember, the Methodist Church in that community, known as Davis Chapel, had a custom of holding a religious service every

Christmas Day. I went to the church that morning, found a good congregation, largely of young people. The request was made by the leader, "All who will take an active part in the services, come toward the front." Most all in the congregation moved toward the front. I kept my seat, for while I had joined the church and been baptized, I was in no condition to take an active part in the services.

The services began as follows: Reading the Scriptures, a number of enthusiastic songs, a cyclone of prayer, followed by another red-hot song. They then threw it open to an old-fashioned testimony service, and to my dying day, and I trust through all eternity, I never shall forget that service. The boys and girls, young men and women, with whom I had associated from my childhood, with tears in their eyes and shining faces, divine eloquence, told of their repentance, their faith in God, their sky-blue conversions, their perfect soul-rest, peace and joy in the Holy Ghost. My soul cried out within me and said, "That is what I must have."

I spent a restless night in honest prayer, under deep conviction. The next day the meeting was transferred to a log schoolhouse where it had been running for weeks. They ran all-day services and a large portion of the night, for they began at nine o'clock in the morning, ran till twelve, opened the afternoon service at two, having dismissed those who wanted to go, some went home, others remained.

I went to the woods nearby, fell down by an old white oak stump, where I made my first audible

CONVERSION 43

prayer. I cried two hours to God for mercy and went back to the schoolhouse at two o'clock and fell at the altar again at a backless bench known as the MOURNERS' BENCH. Thank God for an OLD-FASHIONED MOURNERS' BENCH! After the afternoon service, I returned to my old white oak stump, fell on my knees before God, still crying to Him for salvation. At the night service, as soon as the altar call was made, I fell at the altar, it being crowded as usual with truly penitent sinners. The power of God was so manifest on the people that they had no need of a pracher. Such conviction rested on the unsaved they needed no preaching or exhorting to get them to the altar. The Christians sang, shouted, talked and prayed with mourners; mourners with streaming eyes and agonizing with God, resulting in constant victorious shouts till no one could possibly tell who was in charge of the meeting, for the power of the Holy Ghost had so dominated the entire presence.

I made up my mind on Christmas morning while sitting in church that I would never stop seeking till I found God. The next morning as I started for service I told God that I would never eat or sleep till I found rest for my soul; that being nine o'clock the twenty-sixth of December fifty-three years ago. So in the night service at nine o'clock with an empty stomach, a weary body, a perplexed head, a heart almost in despair, I could say with David, "The pangs of hell gat hold upon me." In this moment of almost despair a young lady cousin of mine came to me amidst the noise and confusion and said, "Look up, John, and trust God." I threw my eyes upward and my faith Godward and instantly sprang to my feet saying, "I have it, I have it!"

I went immediately to an old uncle of mine, threw my arms around his neck, for he was an unconverted church member, and said to him, "Uncle Jesse, come and give your heart to God." He went with me to the altar and prayed through to God. And the last time I heard from him he was preaching the everlasting Gospel of Jesus Christ. That was the first soul I ever led to God. The next night I went home and instituted the family altar, at which God poured out His Holy Spirit on my soul and put such conviction on mother, my two brothers and two sisters that some of them were saved immediately; the rest later in life. Since that time mother and one brother and two sisters have died victoriously. From that night till now, the sole object of my life for these fifty-three years has been to live daily in fellowship with God, and lead others to Christ.

My conversion was so clear and satisfactory that it seemed to me the devil had almost gone out of the business of tempting men. I shall never cease to thank God for an old-fashioned, know-so, sky-blue, never-to-be-forgotten conversion, that has remained with me for over a half century. Not a day in that time that I have not had the consciousness that I was a child of God. When I look inward, backward, forward and upward, the most precious thought of my life is, "I have not given the devil a day's work in fifty-four years, but have spent them all in delightful service to God." To Jesus shall all the glory be given, for I have made many mistakes.

There are two supernatural works of grace wrought always instantaneously in the human soul by the Holy Ghost, i. e., regeneration (or the New Birth) and entire sanctification. Regeneration is the greatest work ever wrought in the human soul because it translates the soul out of death into life; out of darkness into light; from the power of Satan unto God. This radical transition is the greatest change that ever comes into a human life, except the one from earth to heaven. And to say that this can take place in a human experience without the soul having a conscious knowledge of it, is unthinkable to the conscious, sincere soul that wants to know God. For the Holy Spirit, who sheds abroad the love of God in the human heart, always witnesses to the same. "For the Spirit Himself beareth witness with our spirits that we are the children of God."

In the Holy Scriptures, the New Birth (or birth from above) and Regeneration are used as synonyms. John 3:3, "Except a man be born again, he cannot see the kingdom of God." The basis, or necessity of the New Birth (regeneration) is the lostness of man. God made man in His own image and likeness. Genesis 1:26, "God said, let us make man in our own image, after our likeness." So God created man in His own image and placed him in the Garden of Eden to cultivate it and to multiply and replenish the earth, and, as a free moral agent, in full fellowship with God, they walked and talked together. He gave him the privilege to enjoy all the fruit of the Garden except the Tree of Knowledge of Good and Evil, saying unto him, "The day thou eatest thereof, thou shalt surely die,"—spiritual, physical, and eternal death, i. e., spiritual death, separation from God; physical death, the result of sin; eternal death, the final result of sin. Adam, in exercise of his free moral agency, through the temptation of Satan, disobeyed God and brought himself and the whole human family under the condemnation of God and the destructive influences of sin. God could not have made man in His own image, as a free moral agent, capable of obeying His laws without a counter-capability of disobeying them. Satan, a fallen angel, the enemy of God and man, in his satanic shrewdness, said to the first pair, the federal head of the human family, "The day thou eatest thereof thou shall *not* surely die" and succeeded in making them believe his lie instead of God's truth. He erased the likeness and image of God from the human soul and stamped on it his own diabolical image, and imparted unto him a fallen nature, corrupt and *desperately wicked* instead of the nature of holiness which he had received from God. This constitutes the basis or ground of the New Birth.

Regeneration is the re-lifting of the human soul, hitherto dead in trespasses and sins. Regeneration is therefore the focal doctrine of our holy Christianity; for without it all other doctrines are a failure; but with it all other doctrines succeed. Therefore, it is the central doctrine of Redemption. The negative side of regeneration is justification. This takes place in the mind of God in heaven, whereby a man's past sins are all taken away. Regeneration is the positive side of salvation; it is a supernatural work of grace wrought in the human heart by the Holy Ghost and is the basis of all other states of grace here and hereafter. The evidences of the New Birth are as follows:

(1) The burden of sin removed: Matthew 11:28. "Come unto me all ye that labor and are heavy laden, and I will give you rest."

(2) Peace with God: Romans 5:1. "Therefore being justified by faith we have peace with God through our Lord Jesus Christ."

(3) Joy in the Holy Ghost: Romans 5:2. "By whom also we have access by faith into this grace wherein we stand and rejoice in hope of the glory of God."

(4) Love and fellowship for God and His people: 1 John 1:7. "But if we walk in the light as He is in the light, we have fellowship one with another and the blood of Jesus Christ, His son, cleanseth us from all sin." This passage clearly teaches the unmistakable Christian fellowship between man and man and God and man.

(5) An increased love for the Bible and all subjects bearing on our Holy Christianity.

CHAPTER IV.

CALL TO THE MINISTRY.

My call to the ministry was one of the indisputable evidences of a genuine case of salvation; for, as soon as I was converted I had a longing in my soul to lead others to Christ. The call to the ministry is a divine call; and in no sense a professional call—as are the ordinary calls of life. No man should dare enter the ministry of the Gospel of Jesus Christ (1) without a genuine case of know-so salvation; and (2) no man is prepared to preach the full Gospel, without the baptism with the Holy Ghost: Luke 24:49, "And, behold, I send the promise of my Father upon you: but tarry ye in the city of Jerusalem until ye be endued with power from on high." (3) No man should dare to enter this sacred calling without a definite call of God.

My advice has always been, to those who felt themselves called to the ministry: "Do not preach if you can help it; i. e., if the woe of God is not on you. On the other hand, preach or die, if the call of God *is* on you: for a failure to obey God's call, endangers your own soul; and, possibly, the salvation of many other souls." For example, I have in mind a man near my own age, who was saved and called of God to preach, in the same meeting in which I was saved. He failed to obey God, and is today a man wrecked in soul, mind, body, and life. He has failed to meet his obligation to himself, to man, and to God; and is one of the most miserable men I know, his past being a stupendous failure, his present experience miserable, his future hopeless for this world and the one to come. In a recent interview with him, he verified every statement I have made concerning him. God pity the man who has *heard* the call of God and failed to answer it! But, with stronger emphasis, I say: God pity the preacher *without* a divine call; for that means a failure to himself, and the possible damnation of the souls to whom he preaches.

I have in mind two splendid, prosperous business men, who, in their early lives, were saved and called to the ministry, but failed to answer the call; and, while men today of fine business habits and large worldly possessions, they are miserable when they reflect on the fact that their lives have been largely a failure in helping men to God: because they failed to obey God in the great work of winning souls to Christ—the greatest work that God has ever permitted a human soul to enjoy in this world.

My call of God to preach the Gospel of Jesus Christ was as clear as my call to repentance and salvation and the witness of the Spirit to my conversion, which all the forces of earth and hell combined have never made me doubt. Glory to God! Immediately after my conversion I began to work for God with individual souls, in revivals, assisting in meetings whenever I got an opportunity. Owing to my zeal as manifested in the private circle, in public, in prayer and testimony and exhortation, people soon began to say, "That boy will preach." I had felt the call of God to work for Him; and, possibly, to preach for Him: and, when I heard the statements of others and had the impression that God was calling me to preach, I argued the case with both myself and God; urging that I had neither the talent nor the educational equipment for such a high calling. I went on that way for months, till I became a miserable young man every time I would think of it; the happier I would get, the more forcibly I would feel the call. I continued to wrestle with God on the subject—often counseled with preachers and other godly friends; and still my mind was perplexed and my heart heavy.

One evening, about twilight, after a hard day's plowing, in constant prayer and meditation as to my call and future work, I made up my mind (as to my "call"); when I went to my accustomed place of secret prayer, which I sought three times a day, in some quiet place on the farm, where I felt free to pray as long and loud as I pleased—i. e., till I heard from heaven. I went on my knees, saying, to God: *"I must have this settled once for all. If I am not to preach, do not bless and make me happy at all."* (For, in those days, we *"green country folks"* never *counted* a "blessing" unless it *made us happy*: and I must confess that I am not much wiser yet! For a preacher who does not get happy under his own preaching will not make others happy, get sinners converted, or believers sanctified.) I also said to God: "If I *am* to preach, *bless* me so *much* that I

CALL TO THE MINISTRY 51

shall *never doubt* my call to the ministry." I do not know how long I was on my knees; but when I came to my *consciousness* I had *hollowed* myself hoarse, and was saying in a whisper, "*It is settled! It is settled!*" Thank God, from that moment to this, I have never doubted my divine call to the ministry. And, after fifty-two years of preaching the everlasting Gospel of Jesus Christ and Him crucified, I can say out of a glad heart and a restful mind, that I have *never regretted*, for one moment, my call to the ministry and my place in the Methodist Itinerancy; but, on the contrary, my heart leaps with joy when I think my Lord and Saviour saw *enough in me to honor* me with a *place* in His *holy ministry* and to *let* me preach this wonderful Gospel with an eye single to His glory—with one single motive and happy heart, for the glory of God and the salvation of men.

Notwithstanding, I suppose I would be correct in saying that I have had the usual tests of the minister of the Gospel; but I will say also, to the glory of God, and for the comfort of my brethren in the ministry, and the people to whom I have preached, and especially to the young, prospective preachers and missionaries, that, if I had a *thousand years to live in this world and a thousand lives to live*, I would *gladly consecrate* them *all* to *God*. I expect to praise Him through all eternity for my fellowship with Him here; and for the splendid fellowship He has permitted me to have with His blood-washed children, both ministers and Spirit-filled men and women in the different ranks of the church; and for the fact that, under God, my poor ministry has led hundreds to Christ, yea, through those whom I have trained, even thousands; and I trust in the future, through them, tens of thousands may yet be led to God after my work on earth is done, before Jesus comes again to receive His blood-washed Church unto Himself.

I was told by an old minister—when I was a young man—that, when I should become old, full of the fearful responsibilities of the work of the ministry and the multiplied privations through which a minister is called to pass, I should regret ever having become a preacher of the Gospel. It was said in the presence of my prospective wife; and, when we were alone afterwards, she asked me if that was the judgment of all ministers. I answered her, "No." I said then, that if he felt as he expressed himself, he ought to cease to preach at once. Now that *I* am a *happy* old man, I want to say to the glory of God and for the encouragement of the young life, that God has been in *no* sense a *disappointment* to me; but in *every* sense has been *more* to me than I had *expected;* and, through His infinite kindness, mercy, and leadership, has made life a *beautiful* one to me. Oh, that I could *express* to young life the *in*expressible pleasure which I have in my meditative moments! The pleasure in *in*trospecting my own heart, my own experience; in *re*trospecting the days that are gone; and, thank God, in *pro*specting the days that are to come. If Heaven is any *better* than

CALL TO THE MINISTRY

this, I'll leave no stone unturned between this and Heaven, that is in my power to turn! I am now associated with Asbury College, my first college-child: where hundreds of bright men and women are preparing for the ministry, missionary work, and other lines of labor for God; where I have the exalted and inexpressible privilege of public and private association with these; and where I often pour out my heart to God in prayer, sermon and exhortation, with, I believe, the real sympathy and love, not only of the student-body, but of the President and Faculty which I regard as one of the greatest possible privileges of an "old man."

CHAPTER V.

EDUCATIONAL STRUGGLES.

As a child my literary education was wholly neglected; so my intellect long lay dormant, and was hard to awaken to the full consciousness of its normal aspirations and possibilities. My conversion at the age of sixteen introduced me not only to a new realm of the spiritual world, but also to a new physical and mental world; and then I began to have a real vision of the true development of body and mind, as well as of soul—which is normal education. And, from that moment to this, such has been my ideal of correct education. I am sure that this ideal was given me through the divine illumination of the Holy Spirit and has meant more to my life and work, educationally and religiously, than all other things.

No one can have a correct idea of real education, who has not caught his vision from God. "Every good gift and every perfect gift is from above, and cometh down from the Father of Lights, with whom is no variableness, neither shadow of turning." (James 1:17). Higher, as well as rudimental education, in all ages and in all countries, has largely been lop-sided. Grecian and Roman games and races and gladiatorial fights, as well as our own modern football and pugilistic duels, where the physical is developed to the neglect of the mental, moral and spiritual, makes a man beastly, in both his instincts and his practices. On the other hand, to develop the intellectual to the neglect of the physical and spiritual, dwarfs the body and soul: and results in dead Intellectualism, Rationalism, or Infidelity. To educate the soul to the neglect of the body and mind, leads to Fanaticism. God, who made the body of the dust of the earth and breathed into its nostrils the breath of life, (i. e., physical, mental, spiritual, and eternal,) meant for it to be kept in perfect harmony with Himself and His laws. And no education is complete—or Christian—that fails to conform to the will of God and to His laws.

Immediately after my conversion and call to the ministry, I began to make some preparations to preach, by working awhile and going to school awhile, until I became sufficiently equipped to teach in the public schools. Then I had an intense longing for a college education. At this vital juncture, Rev. T. F. Taliaferro, member of the Kentucky Conference, and his excellent wife, came into our country on their second circuit. I had not before met such a cultivated and attractive young couple; for my environment had been quite different from theirs. I often sought their company, and was permitted to have splendid fellowship with them, for they seemed to see something in me that might possibly be developed. They became my substantial friends, and did all in their power to advise, instruct and encourage me, being to me in a most emphatic sense a true brother and sister in the Lord. Owing to their kindness, attractiveness, and interest which they took in me, there sprang up between us a love and fellowship that has never abated. They called me John, and I called them Tom and Mary; and this has obtained through life. Their culture, refinement, cordiality, beautiful Christian lives, and kindness shown me, intensified my desire for an education. And through their advice I entered Kentucky Wesleyan College at Millersburg, Kentucky, in February of 1874. Under God they had much to do with my preparation for the ministry, and whatever usefulness I may have had in the world.

I entered the Kentucky Wesleyan College with fear and trembling; for it was the first college I had ever seen. I was the first boy that had ever gone to college from our neighborhood. It seemed to be a greater undertaking to me then, than my trip to the Old Country seventeen years ago! I rode horseback about thirty miles, with a friend who led my horse back home. When we came in sight of the college buildings my heart seemed to displace my Adam's apple!—not with stage fright, but with college fright.

One of the seniors said to me next morning: "Mr. Hughes, what course do you expect to take?" I answered: "I do not know what you mean." He said, "Freshman, Sophomore, Junior, or Senior?" I replied: "I do not know, all I know is that I am going to enter school in the morning." For I had never heard of a college curriculum, and did not know the bottom of the course from the top.

I went alone into the chapel service, trembling from head to foot, with a perplexed head and an unquiet heart. So self-conscious was I that I felt sure that the president, faculty, and student body had their eyes on *me*, saying in their hearts: "This is the greenest proposition we have ever struck!" And I was in no condition to deny it.

Since then I have learned that every man is an *ignoramus*, concerning everything that he does not know. But with all my normal belligerency, I kept perfectly quiet—which my friends know—was an abnormal condition.

At the close of the chapel service, the president asked me to see him in his office. That intensified my fright; and, when he asked my name, I succeeded in telling him, but when he asked my age, my memory "played hooky" on me, and, in my inexpressible embarrassment, and consequent bewilderment, I gave him the wrong date.

My course having been assigned me, I got my books and entered my classes. I did my utmost to prepare my lessons thoroughly. In some of them I did fairly well; in others, very poorly—especially in general history. I could not well remember *dates, names,* and *facts,* which prevented me from becoming an expert historian, as was evident to my teacher and my fellow students! I would often spend three hours in the preparation of my history lesson, and go to the class and practically fail on it. Often a boy of fifteen years, who had enjoyed early educational advantages, would make a perfect recitation, saying to someone in my hearing: "I spent only thirty minutes on this lesson." And the devil—who is always on the job—would whisper in my ear to discourage my heart, saying: "You have no sense, and can never get an education; give it up and go home; split rails, plow corn, worm tobacco—these are the only things that you are capable of doing." I would go to my room with this dejected spirit, cry, pray, and do my utmost again to prepare a respectable recitation.

One morning at two o'clock, after a day of great dissatisfaction with my school work, in great despondency—not to say hopelessness—having rolled and tossed in my bed until that late hour of the night, I got up and took a long walk out to an old cemetery, feeling it would be more congenial to my feelings to be placed among the dead in the cemetery, than to continue through life as I felt that night. As I walked back to the college, I made up my mind that I would go back to my room, pack my trunk, go home next morning, and give up life's objective in absolute despair. But, as Providence would have it, just as I reached the stone fence in front of the college, God came on the scene, calling to my memory a statement that some of my neighbor boys made the day I left home for college: "John won't stick." The Holy Spirit thus so stirred the depths of my manhood and highest aspirations that I said to myself: "God helping me, I *will* stick to the calling and leading of God, at any cost; and I will do all that is in my power from this moment to make a real man, and strive to make the world better." I then put my hands on the stone fence in front of the college, jumped over, and ran back to the college hurriedly, with the determination to do my best to bring out all there was within me.

This I have called my "Rubicon." Its memory has served for encouragement to my own heart, when dark shadows have come; and I have used it to the encouragement of scores of young men and women undergoing similar experiences as college students, in the twenty-four years that I spent as president of colleges. I have had scores of them, first and last, from the age of twenty to thirty-seven, in their testing moments, combating poverty and early disadvantages, with streaming eyes, say: "There's no use for me to stay in school, for I cannot learn anything." Through this story I have just related, with scarcely a single instance to the contrary, I have seen them go away hopeful, with smiles on their faces, saying: "If you came through such difficulties as those, I'll do my best to take your advice; and hope to make something yet of myself."

I had a case of discouragement, which I shall relate for the sake of some discouraged one who may read these lines. He was a man of family, about thirty-five years old, weighed about two hundred pounds, of very meager rudimentary education, with a clear call to the ministry, and a genuine case of conversion and sanctification. He had entered school and was making commendable progress; but his wife vigorously opposed his preaching, fearing that they might starve. At the close of chapel service one morning, he came to my office, crying like a boy of ten years. I said to him: "What on earth is the matter?" He replied: "I have to quit school, for my wife is so dissatisfied that I cannot study. She says that if we enter the ministry we shall starve." "Is that your only trouble?" I asked. "Yes," he replied. I then said: "Put your hand in mine, and we will tell the Heavenly Father about it." We did so, and got the assurance that God would take care of the case; we had asked Him to give her no peace until she sought the salvation of her soul, and agreed to co-operate with her husband in the work of the ministry. He left me with a smile on his face and assurance in his heart. A few days later he said: "My wife is under intense conviction, and can scarcely eat or sleep." I urged, "We will hold steady." A day or two later I saw him coming up the walk to the college, with a shine on his face that indicated triumph. I said, "What has happened?" He said, "Wife was gloriously saved last night, and says now that she will gladly do all she can to make my ministry a success"—which she did, and they have been a splendid success in the ministry.

If my life has been worth while to the world in any educational sense, it is because the Holy Spirit gave me this conception of real education, when He called me from a life of sin to a life of righteousness. And, with increasing light, He called me to preach His everlasting Gospel. And finally He gave me a vision and a call to *Christian Educational Work*.

EDUCATIONAL STRUGGLE

Any success I may have had in my life-work, is attributable to God; and all the mistakes and failures which I may have made or had, are attributable to my own head and heart: all of which I most heartily deplore, for doubtless they have often marred the work God meant me to do. Yet I profoundly thank and praise Him for the privilege, in a small way, of being a co-worker with Him on educational and religious lines.

Notwithstanding my many difficulties in entering college, and its first year's obstacles to be overcome, I will say I think it is due to myself and those who will read this book, that after my first year in school I got adjusted to the situation, and took on new courage and nerved myself for the conflict, and made good the rest of my school life. I had to work my way through school, and of course, that took some of my strength and time. I was once in debt for a suit of clothes and wrote to my mother to ask a near relative of mine if he would send me the money to pay the debt I would pay him when I got home and made the money. His classic reply was, "Tell John that he can paddle his canoe and I will paddle mine." That brought all of my *manhood* to the *front* and I said *"By the grace of God I will do it."* That has meant much to my life.

CHAPTER VI.

AS A PASTOR.

From the days of the Apostolic Fathers down to the present time, the pastor, as one of the divinely constituted orders of the Christian ministry has played a prominent and important part on the stage of ecclesiastical history. He is a connecting link between the laity and the hierarchy. More than the higher official dignitaries of the church he comes in direct contact with the practical problems of the people. He marries the living, buries the dead, teaches the young, comforts the aged, consoles the disconsolate, moulds public sentiment, maintains morality and proclaims the unsearchable riches of the glorious gospel of Jesus Christ.

The pastorate as an institution has been adorned and dignified by a grand galaxy of able and distinguished men. We may point with pardonable pride to the great outstanding pulpiteers of the world. In the course of Christian history we may mention John Chrysostom, Aurelius Augustine, Martin Luther, Hugh Latimer, John Knox, John Calvin, Jeremy Taylor, Richard Baxter, John Bunyan, Jean Massillon, Jonathan Edwrads, John Wesley, George Whitefield, Rowland Hill, Timothy Dwight, Robert Hall, Christmas Evans, Thomas Chalmers, Edward Irving, Charles Hodge, Henry Newman, Horace Bushnell, Thomas Guthrie, Matthew Simpson, Henry Ward Beecher, Alexander Maclaren, John A.

AS A PASTOR

Broadus, T. DeWitt Talmage, Chas. H. Spurgeon, Phillips Brooks, and in more recent times, Frank W. Gunsaulus, Newell D. Hillis, J. Wilbur Chapman, G. Campbell Morgan, J. H. Jowett, A. C. Dixon, George Stuart, George F. Truett, Frank Norris, Mark A. Matthews and many others.

The pioneer preachers of the Methodist ministry in America have made a record almost unparalleled in the annals of human history. As sanctified circuit riders they saddled their horses and blazed the trail of civilization. They climbed rugged mountains, penetrated trackless forests, crossed swollen streams and marched onward through summer's heat and winter's cold, amid falling rains and driving snows in order to carry the gospel evangel to the early settlers of the great western wilderness.

"It is the glory of the Methodist Church," said John B. McFerrin, "that her ministers are always found on the frontiers."

When John W. Hughes joined the Methodist Conference in 1876 the days of the early pioneer preachers in the great middle west had practically past, but the far-reaching effect of their faithful ministry remained. Similar conditions, however, existed in some of the outlying rural and neglected districts of the country. Dr. Hughes commenced his pastoral ministry as a young circuit rider.

When the bishop read out his appointment at the close of the annual conference he accepted it with greater joy and gladness than if he had been called and commissioned as an American consul to some foreign court. He made a splendid record as a pastor. He had initiative, enthusiasm, executive ability and social qualities sufficient to put over propositions and to bring things to pass. His rise in the religious world was rapid, but regular. He went within a few years from a small obscure country circuit to a fine station. The people on the different pastoral charges where he was sent to serve soon recognized that a man of God was in their midst. He was a live wire. His religious enthusiasm was contagious. The laity caught his spirit and fell in line for larger and better things. He became known far and near as a preacher, church-builder, pastor and revivalist. He put his people to work. Wherever he went things had to move. He could not tolerate a cold, dead, formal church. He would rattle the dry-bones in the valley, pray, preach and shout until he heard the sound of agony in the tops of the mulberry trees indicating victory. He believed that a pastor ought to have religion, common sense, natural ability, mixing qualities, love for souls, consecration to his task and the unction and power of the Holy Ghost sent down from heaven.

Dr. Hughes has devoted two chapters in the present volume to his "Pastoral Work." In them the reader will see how he met and solved the difficult problems that confront a young preacher; how he handled that formidable factor of the congregation known as the official board; how he "reached the masses," conducted revivals and reaped a rich harvest in the salvation of souls.

AS A PASTOR

His experience as a pastor covered a period of thirteen years. He found that the pastorate, under the Methodist itinerant system, was a fine and fertile field for the free exercise of his gifts and graces. It trained his mind, tested his mettle, tried his nerve, developed his character and in a word made a man of him. As these years of faithful and efficient service in the pastorate constituted a very important part of his life's work it is perfectly proper to give plenty of space to the narration of the principal events and incidents that occurred during this time.

Dr. Hughes has always been a friend, true and tried, to the pastors. Through his fruitful ministry many young men have entered the pastorate. During his college career he trained many for pastoral work and sent them out to all parts of the world.

ANDREW JOHNSON.

CHAPTER VII.

PASTORAL WORK.

The Kentucky Conference convened in Nicholasville, Kentucky, September, 1876, with Bishop Keener presiding. I was received on trial at this conference, and was assigned to my first pastoral charge, Springport circuit, in Henry and Carroll counties, containing four appointments. My predecessor was old Brother Quissenberry (known by the people as "Uncle Cush.)" He was a remarkably popular man, loved by saint and sinner, church members and outsiders. For a time I made his house my home and received from him and his excellent wife a father's and mother's love and advice. They introduced me to my new constituency. One day when the ex-pastor introduced me to an old lady she scanned me from head to foot and said, "Is anyone with you?" I answered, "No, this is all there is of it."

A careful inventory of my assets and liabilities were three sermons and two old fashioned tunes. For in those days the churches had no musical instruments and the preacher often had to conduct the music. At my first quarterly meeting I told my presiding elder to be sure and get an old song for I would probably have to lead the music, but he gave out a new one and I pitched a common-meter song to a short-meter tune. Of course I had to double up on it, which tremendously embarrassed me and did not make the most harmonious music. As we retired from the church the presiding elder in a jovial manner said, "Your singing today reminded me of a duck eating two mouthsful at once." To continue my inventory, I was just out of college with a two hundred dollar school debt, and had to buy a horse, saddle, bridle, blanket and a pair of saddlebags all on credit so that I might have a way to get to and from my appointments.

I had made up my mind to be a successful pastor, and that meant to me to be a soul winner. I visited from house to house and prayed and talked with my people about the salvation of their souls. Each year I held a protracted meeting at each church on my charge and took a goodly number of people into the church, but, sad to say, had no conversions. The custom of that day in our church, as well as in other churches, was to take people into the church without requiring or expecting a clear case of regeneration and the witness of the Spirit.

All my debts were paid during the year, fifty dollars worth of books secured, a forty dollar suit of clothes, a silk plug hat (which most of the preachers, young and old, wore in those days) and fifty dollars in my pocket with which to begin the new conference year.

The next year I was assigned to the Visalia circuit near Covington, Kentucky. I had something like one hundred additions to the church but no conversions. I built and dedicated a nice church and closed my year's work with what the people considered a successful year.

The Conference met that Fall at Paris, Kentucky, with Bishop Wilson presiding. I was sent to the Ruddell Mills charge, containing three churches which at one time had an aggregation of nine hundred members but were now run down to fifty. I held a protracted meeting at each one of the churches with some encouragement. There were a number of additions to the churches that year.

In the Fall of 1879 I entered Vanderbilt University, and spent a pleasant and profitable year, getting good intellectual training. But my soul longed for food that I did not receive in the college or university. When opportunity presented, I spent the Sundays in preaching with pastors and in schoolhouses around the University, often walking to and from these appointments, glad of the blessed privilege for the sake of my soul and the benefit of others. One day I walked nine miles, preached in the morning and walked home in the afternoon. I had the assurance that God was approving my efforts by making my own soul happy and receiving statements from the people that I had been some help to them. When the faculty found I was so anxious to preach and the people were willing to hear me, the pastors were often referred to me as a young man that was glad to preach whenever he had an opportunity so I was kept preaching much of my time on Sundays.

When I entered Vanderbilt University I had between four and five hundred dollars and owed nothing. I spent it all during the year and had to borrow money to start my next year's work.

PASTORAL WORK

In 1880 Conference met at Lexington, Ky., with Bishop McTyiere presiding. I was assigned to Tollesboro Circuit in eastern Kentucky with four appointments. I entered upon my year's work with an earnest prayer to God and a heart longing for success in soul winning. I had a protracted meeting at each one of my appointments, a goodly number of additions and some clear-cut, old-fashioned conversions. It was my good fortune this year to be in the home of Thomas Putman and his elect wife, two of the truest christians I have ever known. Truly they were a father and mother to the young preacher. Peace be to their memories, for they have long ago entered upon their reward, but they are still in the memory of this preacher, and will continue to be until we meet again. It was said of him during the Civil War when the devil had captured most of the churches and many of the preachers, that a common saying of the public was, "Uncle Tom has the true article," which he never failed to defend and testify to with the boldness of Saint Paul. Among a number of remarkable sayings or utterances of his that have clung to my memory was "I know the Bible is true because it corroborates my experience." This unique statement of my old-sainted friend has followed me in all my theological studies as one of the most significant or original expressions I have met even in theological terminology.

This year was a momentous year to me. Two remarkable things transpired. First, I ceased to be a circuit rider and became a circuit driver by securing a new buggy and harness outfit. Second, I was married the twenty-eighth of July to Miss Mary Wallingford, who was one of the most beautiful women in person and character that I had ever met. I thought so the day of our marriage, and after traveling with her thirty-three years, eight months and nine days I believe that I can safely say that very few pastors have ever had a wife more beautifully adapted to the work of a preacher's wife.

In the Fall of 1881 conference met at Danville, Kentucky, Bishop Keener presided. We were assigned to the Chaplin circuit with three appointments in Nelson and Washington Counties, near the border of the Louisville conference. Immediately after adjournment of the conference, we started as husband and wife to our first appointment with happy hearts and a determination to succeed in the Methodist itinerancy. On arriving at our new home, we were cordially received by the members of our constituency. Finding the parsonage and all three of the churches in a bad state of repairs, we made up our minds at once to do everything in our power to renovate the buildings. We succeeded in building one new church and putting the other two churches and parsonage in good state of repair. I shall never forget when we got our scanty furniture in the little parsonage, and when wife and I sat down at our own table with a meal provided by her own hands, there was a joyful home feeling that had never come to my heart before, that doubtless comes to every new couple at their own table.

We began at once to fill our appointments and to visit from house to house, doing all in our power to find the religious status of our people. My wife was not clear in her conversion and often when we went into a new home I would say to her when alone, "If this man and his wife were saved people they would make great workers in the church and be mightily used of God in helping to save others." My wife would say, "Why do you speak thus? How do you know that they are not saved people?" But later on when she was saved with a sky-blue case of regeneration, she understood why I spoke thus, for I spoke not as a critic but as an earnest pastor anxiously solicitous for the salvation of my flock. No man is competent to fill the place as pastor in the church of God until his own religious experience is such that he will spend and be spent to get the unsaved of his church and outside community to God, and feed the saints of God who are bearing the burdens of the church, and who like himself, have a heart longing for the salvation of sinners and the upbuilding of the church of God. It soon became clear to the pastor and his wife that the charge was in great need of a genuine revival, and God being witness, we made up our minds that we would leave no stone unturned to put the church on a prosperous and healthy basis. So we left no member unvisited in mansion or cabin. This brought the people to church where conviction of the Holy Ghost was such as to make them hunger and thirst for union and fellowship with God.

After getting acquainted with most of the people

of our different churches, I began a revival service at the town church, having made up my mind to have an old-fashioned revival at any cost, and the only way that I knew to bring it about was to preach the old-fashioned gospel, the gospel of sin and damnation to the sinner and righteousness and heaven for the saint. But I was fully aware that that kind of preaching would stir three worlds,—earth, heaven and hell, which it began to do at once. The people told my presiding elder that they were much pleased with the young pastor and his wife but for one thing, and that was that his standard was too high. They implied that I had a zeal, but not according to knowledge. But the Holy Ghost endorsed my standard and put great conviction on the people in and out of the church. They packed the house, gave good attention, and for a solid week I had fourteen persons at the altar every night. But the church, like an invalid mother, did not have health and strength enough to bring forth the unborn child. One man said to me, "Young man, I believe that you are right, if we could only reach your standard," implying that the standard could not be reached. He further added, "I used to hear my old Methodist father talk like you are preaching."

In the midst of the above meeting my first quarterly conference came. My presiding elder was a very superior man intellectually and socially,—an extraordinary preacher and a splendid orator, but not very spiritual. While he was being entertained in the home of one of the principal families of the church, they put before him thoroughly the estimate of their young pastor, saying that he had the qualifications and possibilities of a successful pastor, but to their mind his standard was too high. For a week or more, they said, he had had an altar filled with penitents but would not open the door of the church so that they could become members. He gave me their tale of woe, hoping that he could change my method of running revivals, pleasing the people by taking their sons and daughters into the church instead of holding them continuously at the altar of prayer till they were saved.

My wife was among the penitents at the altar. She had been a seeker for several months. She sought an interview with the presiding elder. After this interview I said to her, "How did you and the presiding elder come out?" Her reply was, "I feel better." For he had told her that her case of salvation was as clear as her husband's, but she was of a different temperament to her husband and would never have the same assurance or demonstration that her husband had; that he was of a nervous temperament and full of demonstration. She saw by the cut of my eye that I didn't believe what he said. Though I fully realized that he was a bigger preacher than I ever expected to make. But my conversion had been so absolutely satisfactory that I was not willing that my life-companion should stop seeking until she had received a like experience.

She said, "What do you think about it?"

I replied, "I am absolutely certain that he was incorrect, for temperament has nothing to do with one's assurance of salvation, when the Holy Ghost has fully saved a soul and witnessed to that important fact." Time and again at our family altar in which she joined me in audible prayer (though unsaved) when I would get happy she would look at me pitifully and say, "Why cannot I feel like you do?"

I said, "You will feel as I do when you get what I have and will need no one's advice, not even from a presiding elder, for the Holy Ghost shall have fully put the matter of your salvation beyond the devil's doubts or the need of man's advice."

That was Friday night preceding the quarterly meeting and I knew that it was my last sermon before the four sermons of the quarterly meeting by the presiding elder and I dreaded the results. For I knew that he believed and taught gradualism in regeneration, which I knew was incorrect. After forty years' study of the Bible and theology I affirm without any fear of contradiction that regeneration and entire sanctification, being the two supernatural works wrought in the human soul, are always wrought instantaneously. With a heavy heart and perplexed head I went to the stable to feed my horse, and while kneeling by a corn pile in my crib in agonizing prayer to God I asked God to give me that night Mrs. Anna Hobbs, a woman that I had been told was the most religious woman in the church. I got the assurance from heaven that she would get to God that night and went to the house and told my wife. She put her arms around me crying and said, "Why didn't you say me?"

I said, "Because you have not gotten to the point of desperation about the salvation of your soul as has Mrs. Hobbs."

For one day during the week as I pronounced the benediction God had owned my message and had given Mrs. Hobbs a clear vision of her lostness and she came and put her hand on my shoulder and said to me with streaming eyes, "Brother Hughes, I am lost. For God's sake pray for me." This pungent conviction had lasted several days and I had felt absolutely certain that her salvation was drawing nigh even before I got the witness of the Holy Spirit that He would save her that night. I went to the church with that assurance. God owned my message. Conviction was stronger than ever. I had no one in the church, not excepting the presiding elder, who could or did aid me in getting the people at the altar through to God. I asked the presiding elder if he would come and aid me. He took a chair, sat down on the inside of the altar, said a few words to a penitent, and watched me in my soul agony trying to instruct and pray these people through. It is a calamity to any church, and a double calamity, to any preacher that cannot lead a penitent to Christ. But, sad to say, they are legion. The services closed with no conversions. The devil, true to his work, said to me, "God disappointed you tonight and did not answer your prayer." Out of the depths of my soul I came back at him saying, "That prayer will be answered tonight, for God does not fail to keep His word."

Next morning while it was yet twilight, I put on my overcoat, went to the home of Mrs. Hobbs and knocked on the family room door. A voice answered, "Come in." I opened the door ajar and said, "I am listening for your report." She was dressing the children. She said, "Come in, for I have heard from heaven an have received what my soul has so long hoped for, and am just arranging to go out in town and tell the story to my neighbors."

She spent the day in going from house to house, including the business houses, with shining face and a God-directed message and testimony until the whole town said, Mrs. Hobbs has something she has never had before, and what she has we all need. She was the entering wedge on that charge to the revival work which followed the next three years amounting to three hundred conversions and many scores of additions to the church. The charge from that time became one of the most vigorous and excellent charges in the conference. The saddest feature, however, connected with this meeting was the result of the presiding elder's four sermons on *gradualism*. I never succeeded in getting conviction back on the people that year.

About the same time the following year I had a gracious revival at the same church. The pastor was sanctified, his wife converted and many other clear conversions and additions to the church. When my wife was converted she went to our presiding elder and said to him, "The temperament of myself and husband are not the same, but I know now for myself that I have the kind of experience my husband has, and for which he so persistently stands." The presiding elder admitted and confessed his mistake, saying: "I was wrong, Sister Hughes, and in my judgment destroyed the best prospect for an old-fashioned revival that I had seen in many years, indeed from my boyhood."

CHAPTER VIII.

PASTORAL WORK CONTINUED.

The conference was held the fall of 1885 at Versailles, Kentucky. I was assigned the Campbellsburg circuit, containing four churches.

At my first appointment I had the assurance that God's hand was on the people, and announced that on Monday night preceding my next appointment I would begin a series of meetings. The time came. The night was dark and rainy. We had left our two children with one of our new members and drove in a buggy two miles to the church over a mud road, which we could not have done had it not been for the almost constant flash of lightning. When we arrived at the church, the rain poured in torrents. The only sign of a congregation was the voice of one man clearing his throat, and I fortunately guessed who it was and said, "Is that you, Will?" (Will Wyatt). He answered, "It is." I said, "Go in and light up and make a fire and we will have a service."

He said he thought to himself what in the name of sense does the man mean to do with but one auditor? After having a few moments chat, knowing him to be a good singer, I said, "Let's have a song."

After the song I said, "Will, have you got religion?"

He said, "No, Brother Hughes, I am sorry to say I haven't."

I said, "I do not know of a better time to get it than tonight."

The rain continued to pour and the lightning to flash. We went on our knees in prayer. My wife prayed, I prayed and then called on Will to pray, and I saw clearly that he was under conviction for sin. We had another song, and wife and myself did all we could to get him through to God, he being our only auditor.

Next morning at ten o'clock he and five others were present. The rain continued to pour. He was converted that morning. He was the entering wedge, for that and the following year, to at least three hundred conversions and scores of additions to the church. His wife was converted a few days later in the wonderful revival that followed. He entered the conference the next fall, of which he is still a member, and through his conversion and ministry, directly and indirectly, five other preachers were saved.

We took these young converts as a blaze of fire to the next appointment. They did splendid work in the great revival in that church. Then adding the converts of the two churches they went to the third church with zeal and a red-hot testimony and we had one hundred conversions in twelve days,—as clear as I ever saw. That gave us additional force from the third church to the fourth which was almost in the center of the charge and something like one hundred converts from the three churches met us on the opening night in the fourth church. After preaching I called for testimonies and from fifty to one hundred responded as rapidly as they could testify. This put pungent conviction on the congregation. But I did not succeed in getting one testimony from the members of that church. One old member followed me out to the carriage that night and said, "What in the name of God will we do?" I replied, "Get on your knees and tell God you will let Him have His way with you." We were expecting a gracious revival, and, thank God, it came.

The wife of one of our leading members who had been talking of the meetings we were having said to her husband, "I am going to have nothing to do with these meetings, for I have heard of the excitement and noise at his other churches." Her husband replied, "Molly, he will get you the first one."

As I entered the church the third night, with a good audience present and still others coming in, she met me half way down the aisle saying, "I thank God I am saved." She said it with great assurance and earnestness. After a song or two I asked for some voluntary prayers. She was the first one to begin. Part of the words of her prayer still remain with me. She said, "Lord, I thank you for salvation. They call this a nigger meeting and all I have to say is if this is a nigger meeting, it is just what I wanted." From that moment she became an enthusiastic worker in the church, in public prayer, testimony and in helping others to Christ.

At our first quarterly meeting the Board of Stewards was discussing the preacher's salary while

PASTORAL WORK CONTINUED

the presiding elder and I were talking over some other matters. They asked me to go back and talk the matter over with them. I was then asked by a member of the Board what salary it would take to support me and my family. I answered, "That is none of your business for I do not ask you men what it takes to run you and your families." They all laughed heartily at my answer, but seemed a little embarrassed, especially the man that put the question. I answered, "All I have to say about it, brethren, is put it where it was last year, and if I do not make it as easy to collect as in former years, and do not fill the bill satisfactorily, I'll be the easiest man to get rid of that you have ever had."

The two years that I spent on the work were increasingly fruitful in conversions, additions, finances, and general welfare of the churches. At the close of my second year they said, "Of course, you are coming back next year?" I replied, "I think it best that I should not (for during that year I had held twelve revivals, including those on my charge); you had better have a man that will stay with you more constantly." They said, "We'd rather have a live man half of the time than a dead man all the time."

In the fall of 1887 the conference met at Covington, Kentucky, Bishop Granbery in the chair, one of my old University teachers (the best teacher under whom I ever sat.) A committee was sent from Carlisle station asking the Bishop to send me to that charge, which he did.

We entered on our work at once with a determination to do our best to please God, help the Christians, get sinners converted to God and added to the church. The opening seemed to be good. My predecessor was an old ex-college president; a splendid cultured Christian gentleman. He said to me one day before he left the charge: "Young man, you are known in the conference as a revivalist, and I don't wish to discourage you, but I see but little opening for a revival in this town, for during my four years' pastorate, this town has been run over every year with a meeting in each church, gathering in all the outsiders possible. Hence I do not see a great opening on that line." He being an old man, in deference to his age, I did not dispute his word, but I felt in my heart that such a state of affairs indicated more than ever the need of an old-fashioned revival of old-fashioned Holy Ghost religion. For the regular church-joining meeting rarely gets men regenerated. That was sadly so then, and without question, it is so now.

I began at once to preach the lostness of man, justification by faith, regeneration, and witness of the Spirit, assuring my audience that when a man got to God he always had a conscious knowledge of the same. This at once began to put deep conviction, not only on the members of my own church, but on the people in the community in general in and out of the churches.

My first text was, "I determined not to know anything among you, save Jesus Christ and Him crucified." 1 Cor. 2:2. At the close of my sermon, an old gentleman, not a member of the church, but whose wife was, said to me, "Young man, is that a sample of your preaching?" I replied, "I suppose somewhat a fair sample." He replied, "Then something will happen."

I began my protracted meeting about the first of November, doing the preaching myself. I had been holding meetings long enough on my own and other men's charges not to expect easy sailing where the church was not thoroughly alive. But the opposition here, take it all in all, was the most stubborn I had ever found as a pastor. They sent two committees to me asking me not to be so severe on the membership, especially the burden-bearers of the church. The male committee said (for I was then a thin man, a little like Pharaoh's lean kind) "You do not look like a strong man, and we are willing to get you an assistant if you so desire." My classical reply was, "It takes a lean dog for a long race." They went home in a good humor, but rather crest-fallen.

A day or two later we were visited by a like committee of the female part of the church. They assured me that I was making a fine impression upon the church and community, but the leader continued saying, "We think that you are making a mistake in being so hard on the standbys in the church and think you had better touch up the lives of the young people who are so much given to worldliness and general amusements." I assured them that I would look after that matter later. I thanked them for their interest in me and I told them that I felt I had the unmistakable assurance that God was leading me on the right line. They left in a similar condition to the former committee, so far as I could judge.

I was having two hundred to hear me in the morning service and the house and gallery packed at night. I went into the church that night, not only from my knees in agonizing prayer, but with divine assurance that I was pleasing God and would ultimately break through all doubt and opposition and have a gracious revival. I generally gave a short talk on the happenings of the meeting before my sermon. That night I told my audience that I had been visited by two *venerable committees*, male and female, and I appreciated their kindness, and that honesty required me to state to them publicly and their neighbors here assembled that in my deliberate judgment I knew more about how to run a real religious revival than all this town put together, judging from the indications I had come in contact with thus far. That I didn't have commercial sense enough to wrap up a pound of soda, banking sense enough to keep books, lawyer's sense enough to instruct them in law, doctor's sense enough to practice medicine, but that I had been used in the hands of God for more than a dozen years in leading hundreds of sinners to Christ and felt sure that we would have a soul-saving meeting before the meeting closed.

Each day and night increased both conviction and opposition. The final court of appeals made to

PASTORAL WORK CONTINUED

remedy the mistakes of their young pastor was their presiding elder who chanced to pass through the town on his way to one of his appointments. They said to him: "You have ruined us. Our preacher has preached until he has discouraged us all. We wish you would see him and see if he won't somewhat change his plans or methods." His reply was, "You do not know him. He first feels assured that he has the mind of the Lord and he will carry out His plans at any cost." So he touched his horse with a whip and left them in their despair.

One of the members of the church left the town on some business, perfectly indignant at the way things were going. We knew that he left to get away from conviction for sin. We got down on our knees and prayed him back home. He returned the next week. He at once said to his wife, "How is our preacher getting along?" She replied, "Worse and worse." He said, "I wish that I could pray, I would ask God to give him some common sense." Which, when I heard I said, "Amen." For I had never known a man *overloaded* with common sense, and I certainly felt the need of more and more of it. He came to church that night. I said to my wife: "When you take your seat in the choir, while I am on my knees in prayer, look over this large congregation and see if you can locate this man, and if you cannot when I rise and look at you, shake your head. If you can locate him, nod your head." For I had a certain sermon I wanted to preach for his benefit and some others in the church. My text was "Be sure your sin will find you out." That sent him home with an arrow in his heart. And after a thoughtful, restless and prayerful night while sitting in front of his fire next morning he was gloriously saved. He came to church that morning. At the close of the sermon I called for volunteer prayers and he responded. It being a new voice, I did what the Bible told me to do, "Watch and pray" until I discovered who it was. I was absolutely certain from his prayer that he had found the Lord. When we arose from our knees I said, "If anybody wants to tell what God has done for your soul, you are at liberty to do so." He rose and began at once to tell a red-hot, old-fashioned, sky-blue conversion, which I am sure no one in the house doubted.

After a number of testimonies from other persons, another prominent member of the church arose and said, "I love God. I am trying my best to live a Christian. I want you to pray for me." I at once dismissed the audience, stepped to him, put my hand on his shoulder and said to him, "Are you satisfied with your conversion?" He looked at me plaintively and said, "No. I want to see you and have a talk with you." I said, "Come to the parsonage at three o'clock and we will have a talk." He came at the appointed hour and I interviewed him with great care and earnestness, for I know no question so vital for a man to settle as his present and eternal relation to God. So I said to him, "Tell me your story as to yourself and relation to the meeting." (For we had been fellow students in two institutions of learn-

PASTORAL WORK CONTINUED

ing and had a kindly feeling and respect for one another.)

He said, "The first week of your meeting I heard you only at night and ridiculed your sermons and methods all day to those who came into my office (for he was a lawyer) and those whom I met elsewhere. The second week you were so persistent and seemed to be so determined that you convinced me that there was something in what you preached. I gave you close and serious attention at night and have been thoroughly convinced that you are preaching the gospel and a salvation that my soul hungers and thirsts for, and I am a candidate for it at any cost." I said, "Brother, it is going to cost you something. Are you willing to pay the price?" He answered, "I am." I said, "Are you willing as a prominent member of the church and official board if you do not find peace with God before the night service to go to the altar and seek it as all other men have had to find Christ?" For no man has ever found Christ without meeting God at His altar somewhere. He said, "I am and will be at the altar tonight."

When the invitation was given he was the first one at the altar. It being crowded, he did not get through that night, but was at the ten o'clock service next morning. At the close of the sermon he came back to the altar again. Many had prayed through that night and morning. He said to me at the altar just after twelve o'clock, "I wish you would dismiss the audience and you and your wife remain with me," which we did for a time. We felt sure that he would get through to God soon. We separated, praying constantly for him and expecting to hear a favorable report. Wife and I were out taking dinner with one of our members that day. Having separated at the church he went from the altar to his office to send away an important document that he had overlooked. While trying to unlock his complicated safe lock the power of God came upon him assuring him that his sins were all taken away and that his soul had received perfect assurance that he was a child of God. He shouted all over his office, forgetting all about the document. He then went to the parsonage in the pursuit of his pastor and wife, whom he learned were out dining that day. He left word that he had found God and expected to spend the afternoon in telling it to his neighbors.

When the night meeting came on I felt it would be a wise course to let him tell his own story to the audience. He was a lawyer and a man of great quietness, undemonstrative, and in whose life all believed. The audience was surprised to hear him testify that up to this day his church life had been unsatisfying, but now he had obtained perfect satisfaction. In his lawyer-like way he gave the facts concerning his past church life, contrasting it with the perfectly assured Christian life received that day in his office about one o'clock. This put the entire town to thinking and saying, "If this splendid exemplary churchman needed to get to God surely most of the town needed real Bible salvation." His speech was received and considered most thoughtfully and seriously and had more influence upon the town than any preacher's sermon could have had. That man lived consistently in his church and in his political life. He was a circuit judge, and had the confidence of both his religious and political associates. He died a victorious death when a comparatively young man.

The doctor aforementioned who had left the town in order to get rid of the influence of the meeting gave a talk the same night, saying to his neighbors, "You all know that I have had more evil influence upon the young men of this town than perhaps any other man in it, and you know that I am conscious of that sad fact. Now that God saved me the other morning at my fireside I know it just as consciously as I know I have been a sinful man and led others into the wrong. Now by the grace of God I am going to make an earnest effort to help save the young men of this town." He was elected as Sunday school superintendent and made one of the most successful that I had ever known.

The above mentioned brethren proved to be true yoke-fellows the two years I remained there with about 150 others that were saved during my pastorate, and with scores of additions I left the church in a healthy spiritual and financial condition. It was one among the best stations of the Kentucky Conference.

CHAPTER IX.

SANCTIFICATION.

The following expressions, most of them biblical, have the same significance. Entire Sanctification, Baptism with the Holy Ghost, Christian Perfection, Holiness, Perfected Holiness, Second Blessing, properly so called, Perfect Love, The Rest of Faith, The Second Rest and a Clean Heart.

The word "sanctify" has two distinct meanings: (1) To separate to holy uses or purposes, i. e., vessels of the temple, dedication of church buildings, to set apart men to holy offices or orders, such as deacons, elders, and office of bishop. In John's Gospel 17:19, Jesus says in his sacerdotal prayer, "And for their sakes (his regenerated disciples) *I sanctify myself*, that they also might be *sanctified* through the Truth." He meant to say that "I set myself apart to the world's redemption." For He was the only human being holy by nature.

(2) The second meaning is "to purify or make holy." He prays that His regenerated disciples might be purified or made holy. "Sanctify them through thy truth; thy word is truth." John 17:17, "I pray for them; I pray not for the world, but for them which thou has given me for they are thine." This surely settles the question that they were saved men and not sinners. The word "entire" means whole or complete. Therefore, the expression, "En-

SANCTIFICATION

tire Sanctification" means spiritual wholeness or completeness, viz., a man's spiritual or moral nature is completely restored to the image of God.

In the above passage, Jesus undoubtedly was not praying for sinners to be converted, but for Christians to be sanctified. I Thess. 1:1, "Paul, and Sylvanus, and Timotheus, unto the church of the Thessalonians which is *in God the Father* and *in the Lord Jesus Christ*." Sinners are not "in God the Father" nor "in the Lord Jesus Christ;" therefore, Paul's prayer was for converted men and women that they might be wholly sanctified. Justification rids us of our actual sins. Regeneration re-lifes us. Entire Sanctification destroys the "Old Man" or the "Body of Sin" and fills us with the Holy Ghost. Rom. 6:6, "Knowing this that our old man is crucified with him (not suppressed) that the body of sin might be destroyed."

"The carnal mind is enmity against God, is not subject to the law of God, neither indeed can be." The "old man" and the "carnal mind" mean the same in this epistle and elsewhere in the Holy Scriptures, meaning the fallen or corrupt nature inherited by the fall of Adam, our federal head. This nature or principle cannot be subjugated, therefore must be destroyed or eradicated.

I lived an enthusiastic, happy, regenerated life for thirteen years, working constantly in revivals and preparing myself for college, and as a college and university student, and a member of the Kentucky Conference. I was always under conviction for what was known then as "a deeper work of grace," but now known clearly to mean the blessing of entire sanctification. I did not know what my trouble was for I constantly hungered and thirsted after righteousness. The Holy Spirit, always true to his office work, kept me under constant conviction for the *fullness* of the Gospel of the grace of God. But the doctrine and experience of holiness, were not taught then, so far as I knew. Hence I remained in constant anxiety as to what my hunger meant. In the providence of God, Doctor W. B. Godbey wrote me more than once, desiring to hold a meeting for me, but I heard he was a crank, or half crazy, and did not answer his letters. But he came anyway and volunteered his services to hold a meeting, against my own personal wishes. But after much prayer and thought, I concluded to keep him and let the meeting go on. He preached day and night, almost all the time on "inbred sin and holiness" which I and my people thought was a mistake, but proved in the end that he was God-led. Wife, myself and people gave him a careful hearing as did many of the community, resulting in a gracious revival. Had quite a number of clear conversions, among them was my wife, who had been a constant seeker for about two years. One night he preached on Pentecost from the text, "And they were all filled with the Holy Ghost." I was not a backslider, but a burdened Christian praying and hoping for a deeper work of grace, and the salvation of my people. The power of the Holy Ghost rested upon the preacher, his message and the people. The altar was filled with penitent sinners, crying to God for mercy and while I was talking to a penitent in the audience, I felt I must talk to the people, and as I began the Holy Ghost fell on me and took away my consciousness. I sat down on a bench near by and when I came to consciousness I was saying, *"Lord, it is enough. I can bear no more."* I then believed and still believe that the power of God was so great, it was all my nerves could bear. I heard Brother Godbey say, *"Glory to God, Brother Hughes is sanctified."* I was thus wholly sanctified at Chaplin, Ky., 9 P. M., Dec. 30, 1882. I felt for hours as if I were *floating in a realm of divine ether.* I could say with all my heart, "Heaven came down my soul to greet while glory crowned the mercy seat." I could also say with Peter, "Whom having not seen, ye love; in whom though now you see him not, yet believing, ye rejoice with joy *unspeakable* and *full of glory."* I then understood not only what Peter said about "the unspeakable glory," but also what Paul meant when he said "How that he was caught up into Paradise, and heard unspeakable words, which it is not lawful for man to utter." 2 Cor. 12:4. I understand in his Paradisaical experience he meant to say, *"My experience is inexpressible and full of glory and I could not express it, if I were to try."* No regenerated man can explain his experience to a sinner, and no sanctified man can explain his experience to an unsanctified believer. The Holy Ghost alone can reveal these experiences to the human heart and He alone witnesses to the same. My *call* to *holiness* was as *clear* and *pronounced* as my *call* to *regeneration* and the *ministry*.

I began a revival immediately after my sanctification, at Bardstown, Kentucky. The Holy Ghost wonderfully owned my ministry and peace flowing like a river blessedly filled my soul. I felt then, and feel now, that if Heaven were any more blessed I could not afford to miss it. I became, from that moment, a special soul winner, and for many years was almost constantly in revivals; but as I had not been taught that it was my duty and privilege to witness to the work of entire sanctification the same as regeneration, the witness to it in a measure left me.

For about six years I was almost all the time in revivals on my charges or assisting the brethren in their meetings, preaching, testifying to the new birth and the witness of the Spirit with the constant seal of God on my ministry. One of the ministers with whom I worked said to me, "We believe you have the blessing of entire sanctification." I said to him, "I do not know about that as I have not had the opportunity to study the doctrine." I was then perfectly sincere in my answer, but after much prayer and careful investigation of the subject, I felt sure that I had received a greater fullness from God than I had at regeneration.

In the above meeting, I had the most peculiar experience of my life. One night when the altar was filled with anxious seekers, I felt all at once that my interest in the salvation of men was gone. I did not understand it. If I had given way to my feelings, I would have screamed as a madman. I continued the service to the best of my ability. After dismissing the audience I went to my room, fell on my knees and cried to God for an hour with a perplexed mind and an agonizing soul, asking God what my experience meant. He came back to me with wonderful satisfaction, teaching me, *as God only can teach*, that I was getting my *eyes on myself rather than God*. From that day till this, thank God, that lesson He has never had to repeat, for I live daily under the all-searching eye of God with a definite understanding with Him that without Him I can do nothing.

So I made up my mind that I would not stop investigating, and seeking until I had the *unmistakable witness* of the *Holy Spirit* to my *entire sanctification*. I had always felt, since my conversion, that I was an honest seeker after all that God had for me, for I saw definitely and clearly that after God saved His disciples and sent them out to preach the Gospel, He not only taught, but urged them to seek the baptism with the Holy Ghost; Luke 24:49, "And behold I send the promise of the Father upon you; but tarry ye in the city of Jerusalem, until ye be endued with power from on high." I sought it for ten days, scarcely ate or slept, while I was pastor at Carlisle, Kentucky.

At the close of ten days' constant seeking I went to a holiness convention at Newport, Kentucky, and spent all night in prayer to God the night before I received the baptism, or rather the witness. This took place in the basement of the Methodist Church at Taylor Street, Newport, Kentucky. I received the unmistakable witness that I was wholly sanctified; basing my faith on Hebrews 12:2, "Looking unto Jesus the author and finisher of our faith; who for the joy set before him endured the cross, despising the shame, and is set down at the right hand of the throne of God." I was taught clearly by the Holy Spirit the meaning of this text. The word, *author* means *regenerator* and the word *'finisher'* means *sanctifier* or completer; for entire sanctification means wholeness or completeness. And for the last thirty-seven years I have never seen a day that I have not had the divine assurance that the blood of Jesus Christ, His Son, cleanseth from all sin. 1 John 1:7. "But if we walk in the light, as he is in the light, we have fellowship one with another, and the blood of Jesus Christ, his Son, cleanseth us from all sin." I thank God that it has been my pleasure to preach and testify to this wonderful salvation publicly or privately every day since. It has cost me some very *severe criticisms* and some preferments in my conference relations, closing of many church doors that used to be open to me and my *ministry* when *preaching regeneration only*, because I have insisted on preaching and testifying to the doctrine and experience which the Bishop that ordained me made me promise to *groan after* and expect to receive in this life.

John Wesley, the human founder of the great

FIRST BUILDING AT ASBURY COLLEGE.

SANCTIFICATION 97

Methodist Church said, "God has seemed to raise us up as a church to spread scriptural holiness in these lands." While it cost me much to be true to my vows and convictions, it has kept me a steady and happy Christian, *ready to preach, pray,* or *die.* It has enabled me to lead directly many hundreds to the blessings of regeneration and entire sanctification, and through those whom I have trained, multiplied thousands to the fullness of the Gospel of the grace of God. I am absolutely certain that I shall never have a reason to discontinue preaching and testifying to what I promised in my ordination vows, and reception into the Methodist Itinerancy. These vows are as followes:

"After solemn fasting and prayer, every person proposed shall then be asked before the Conference, the following questions (with any others that may be thought necessary), namely: Have you faith in Christ?" (Meaning, have you been born of the Spirit or are you a child of God?)

"Are you going on to perfection?" (Requiring the answer, "I am.")

"Do you expect to be made perfect in love in this life?" (The pertinent question in answer to this is, "When?" Of course the implication is, "In this life, and the sooner the better.")

"Are you groaning after it?" (Answer,— "I am.")

"Are you resolved to devote yourself wholly to God and His work?" (A correct answer to this question implies a continued, complete *consecration of ourselves* and *all* we *possess* to God daily.)

I am now a mature, not to say, an old man and I want to say to the glory of God that my religious experience is deeper, broader, sweeter and more settled than ever before, and that I often get homesick for Heaven, and if I had a thousand years to live, I would fully *consecrate* them all to *Him* and *His blessed service*. If my end were in sight I would not only suggest, but implore my brethren in the ministry (whom I love as no other class of men) and especially the young men, in the language of Paul, Romans 12:1, "I beseech you therefore, brethren, by the mercies of God, that you present your bodies a living sacrifice, holy, acceptable unto God, which is your reasonable service." Which will lead any soul to the blessed *experience* of *entire sanctification;* which he will naturally and gladly preach and testify to, out of a fullness of a heart filled with the Holy Ghost.

CHAPTER X.

THE ORIGIN OF ASBURY COLLEGE.

College Motto: "Industry, Thoroughness, Salvation."

After twelve years in the pastorate and one in the evangelistic field I received a clarion call to college work. Of all calls this was the most unthought of, unexpected, and undesired. My call to repentance and salvation was gladly received; my call to the ministry was hesitatingly received, because I felt my inability and unpreparedness; my call to holiness and full salvation was earnestly sought for and joyfully accepted. My heart had hungered long and earnestly for something, I did not know what, but when I did obtain it, my soul was thoroughly satisfied. My call to college work was clear, but bewildering as I considered what seemed my utter inability and unfitness. I have had the seal of God upon my ministry in the salvation of hundreds of souls both in the pastorate and evangelistic work, and in my profound love for, and success in both fields of labor, my heart drew back from such an unexpected call. I hoped and prayed that I had misinterpreted the summons and that I might continue the work so dear to my heart,—and in which I had had a good measure of success.

I had seen and felt the need for years of a *real salvation school* where religious young men and women could hold their salvation; and where unsaved and unsanctified students would not only be encouraged, but urged to get saved and sanctified and prepared educationally for their life's work. Those who were fully saved and educationally equipped would be urged by faculty and fellow-students to hold themselves in readiness to say to the Lord and the church, as did Isaiah in his vision of God and His holiness and a lost world in its sin, "Also I heard the voice of the Lord saying, "Whom shall I send and who will go for us? Then said I, Here am I; send me." (Isa. 6:8). No man can have a correct conception of God's holiness and man's unholiness till, like Isaiah, he gets a vision of God. He was an earnest young preacher and, no doubt, felt that he and his people were getting along well religiously, when God's flashlight from Heaven so enlarged his vision as to make him cry out, "I saw also the Lord sitting upon a throne, high and lifted up. Then said I, Woe is me! for I am undone, because I am a man of unclean lips and dwell in the midst of a people of unclean lips, for mine eyes have seen the King, the Lord of hosts." A school where the religious atmosphere might be such that the students would recognize the world's need and willingly obey the Lord's command. "But when he saw the multitude he was moved with compassion on them because they fainted and were scattered abroad as sheep having no shepherd. Then said he unto his disciples, The harvest is plenteous, but the laborers are few, pray ye therefore the Lord of the harvest that he will send forth laborers into his harvest." (Matt. 9:36-38).

THE ORIGIN OF ASBURY COLLEGE 101

I believed then, as I do now, that a rounded and complete education involved a genuine, Christian experience. To educate the body to the neglect of the mind and the soul makes a man beastly. To educate the mind to the neglect of body and soul leads to dead intellectualism. To educate the soul to the neglect of mind and body results in fanaticism. I also believed then, as I do now, that a real Christian school would put the Bible in the curriculum, teaching the history, doctrine and experience of our holy Christianity daily, stressing the teaching of Jesus, "Seek ye first the kingdom of God and his righteousness and all these things shall be added unto you." For many years I had been sending young men and women to colleges, out of my revivals, full of faith and the Holy Ghost to get them prepared for the Master's service. A great per cent of them, as they do now, got their faith destroyed, lost their religious experience and the call of God to the ministry and other Christian work.

One day as I sat in the old Kentucky Central Depot, Lexington, Kentucky, having been from my home in Carlisle, Kentucky, for a month in evangelistic work, God gave me, not only a vision of a real salvation school, but called me to the work. I purchased my ticket for Carlisle, my home. I got on the train, I pulled my hat down over my face so that no one could interfere with my prayer and meditation till I reached my destination. I spent part of the time in the bosom of my family with my wife and three children, but I spent hours each day in my room in agonizing prayer with heavy heart and perplexed mind, hoping in some way to rid myself of what seemed to me a fearful responsibility, one that I was in no way prepared to shoulder. I hoped and prayed that God would relieve me of the burden, but as I could get no relief from that direction, I was hopeful that my wife, who had been so faithful and true to me in my work, both in the pastorate and evangelical fields, would enter her protest against my entrance into this untried field. So I called her to my room. When she came in I was on my face upon the floor praying God to help me break the news to her so as to bring right results. She sat down on the floor by me. I said to her, "I have a matter on hy mind to which I must call your *undivided* attention." With her characteristic quietness and frankness, she said, "I am all ears and eyes and will hear what you have to say." When she gave that answer, which implied her willingness to follow me where God would lead, I burst into tears and told her about my call to college work and how perplexed I was over it. Her unexpected answer was, "When I married you, I did it with the understanding that I would follow you into every line of work to which God called you." I felt then that my last prop had fallen and that I could do nothing but obey God and hope and pray for success in our new divinely appointed field. We at once began to pray and to plan for the beginning of our new project.

The news soon got out that I was about to start a College to be known as a holiness school; that in

THE ORIGIN OF ASBURY COLLEGE 103

connection with the college curriculum the Bible would be placed as a regular text-book; and that its history, doctrines and experiences, as revealed in Bible characters, would be taught and emphasized as other text-books. Also that the work of the day would be opened with an earnest religious Chapel service,—in reading and expounding the Scriptures, singing, praying and testifying as the Lord would lead. Each teacher would be required to open his class with a short invocation by teacher or pupil.

We adopted and followed these plans for twenty-four years of school life; we saw splendid results, not only in the religious life of the student body, but more than ordinary success in all departments of college life. We believed then, and know now, that real piety in the student body has much to do with industry, and honest and sincere investigation in all lines of study and college curriculum. Furthermore, the Divine Author who made both the mind and heart will aid the student who leads a life in conformity with His laws, when he goes to Him daily in honest prayer, as a child to his father, asking him to keep his heart full of love and to illuminate his mind so that he may rightly discover and promote the truth on all lines of investigation and honest research.

When I began to advertise the school, a college president said to me: "What is your *objective?*" I answered, *"A sure enough religious school."* "Have you an announcement of the school?" I handed him my first four-page circular. It began as follows:

Introductory.

Feeling the great need of a distinctively religious school where young men and young women can get a thorough College education under the direction of a faculty composed of men and women wholly consecrated to God, we have decided to open "Kentucky Holiness School" at Wilmore, eighteen miles south of Lexington, on the Cincinnati Southern Railroad, near High Bridge. The school will open September 2nd with three teachers. Other teachers will be employed when the patronage demands it. The main building, for the accommodation of boarders, will not be ready for use until December, but the people of the community have agreed to accommodate all boarders who desire to attend the first term. When arrangements are completed, young men and young ladies will room in separate buildings. We expect the hearty co-operation of Holiness people everywhere. We feel satisfied that the work is of God, and will succeed.

Faculty.

Rev. J. W. Hughes,
Proprietor.
James B. Shockley, A.M., Principal.
Ancient and Modern Languages and Bible.
Miss Sallie Woodyard,
Mathematics, English and Science.
Miss Elma Grinstead,
Music.
Mrs. A. E. Shockley and Mrs. J. W. Hughes,
Home Department.

When he read the introduction to my circular, it offended him. He then said, "What do you mean by *distinctively religious school*?" I answered, " I mean a school in which the doctrines and experiences are taught and emphasized daily so as to lead the young men and women to forsake sin and give themselves wholly to God." His reply to that was, "If you mean that fanaticism called 'sanctification,' we endeavor to destroy it." My reply to him was, "I think you succeed as well as any crowd I ever knew." I said, "Furthermore, we will endeavor, as a faculty, to do all in our power to lead our students to the Bible experiences of regeneration and entire sanctification and to live daily a consecrated, holy life with warm hearts and cool heads, always endeavoring to tear down the works of the devil and to build up the Kingdom of God." I have had no occasion since that day to retract my *Objective*.

At the previous Conference I had retired from the pastorate and entered the evangelistic work. I had built a ten-room house in Carlisle, Kentucky, and located my family there with the expectation of spending my life in that field. I owed no man a cent.

I then began to look out for a location for the school. A Mr. Slicer, at Nepton, Kentucky, who had heard of my project, owned a brick school building in that little town. He offered to donate the building if I would locate the school there. I did not like the location. Rev. W. S. Grinstead, the pastor of the Methodist Church in Wilmore, Kentucky, wrote me to come there and look the situation over. I did so. I found a splendid district of country on the Q. & C. railroad, a hundred miles south of Cincinnati, about two hundred and forty miles from Chattanooga, and on one of the best railroads in the State. I thought then and still think it was a model place to locate the college. A good country, fine citizenship, thrifty farmers, healthful, easily accessible, a quiet country place, no town then, only a few scattering houses, away from all the whirl, confusion and wickedness of city life. I felt impressed that this would be an ideal place in which to put a student in contact with a course of study. The magnificent climate, with picturesque surroundings, with all their charms would be the very place to develop character. Experience has comfirmed my early impressions and convictions.

Brother Grinstead called the following gentlemen together: J. S. Lowry, A. B. Blackford, Robert Scott, Edward Scott, Wm. T. Bourne, Jerome Sparks, and T. B. Handy. I laid my plans before them and said to them, "All things considered, I think you have a splendid location for a college, and, as our beginnings are small, if you will raise sixteen hundred dollars inside of a week, I will return at once and begin the project; and if I should run three years you will get your money back in tuition rather than send your children away to other schools, but I assure you, gentlemen, my plans are to build a school here worth while and to give my life to it." I had in my mind, unless God or the devil interfered with my plans, to put the best energies of

THE ORIGIN OF ASBURY COLLEGE 107

my active life in making the school a complete success, and I would have been there to this day if my plans had not been thwarted. Being sure I was led of God to establish the Institution, it being my college child born in poverty, mental perplexity and soul agony, I loved it from its birth better than my own life. As the days have come and gone, with many sad and broken-hearted experiences, my love has increased. My appreciation of what it has done, what it is doing, and what it promises to do in the future is such that I am willing to lay down my life for its perpetuation.

I returned to Wilmore in compliance with my promise in a week. The required money had been raised and the trade consummated and the college had been launched. And, as a matter of fact, the college has not only been running three years, but thirty-three years, and the parties who helped to project it with their money and sympathy have not only received their money in return in the valuation of their property, but several hundred per cent besides, to say nothing of the education of their sons and daughters, and being instrumental in starting an Institution that is being known and felt around the world.

The thirteenth day of July, 1890, I landed at Wilmore Station with my family and household goods and a bunch of mechanics and began at once to build the first four-room house known as the Boys' Dormitory, which still stands. We located at J. K. Lowry's. He and his inestimable wife proved to be a father and mother not only to myself and family, but to the first students, and, with their excellent sons and daughters, the unfailing friends and supporters of the college. Peace be to their memories! And to the memory of many other friends, whose prayers and loyal support helped to project the Institution; their names are too numerous to mention. God has remembered and honored. I owe to Wm. T. Bourne a special debt of gratitude in the establishment of Asbury and Kingswood Colleges, known to ourselves and God alone.

CHAPTER XI.

ASBURY'S STRUGGLES AND SUCCESSES..

In a short time, the mechanics had completed the four-room dormitory. We moved into this at once while the mechanics began work on what was known as the Girls' Dormitory, afterward, Music Hall.

The second day of September we opened the school in the four-room dormitory, in the two upstairs rooms, with eleven pupils, two literary teachers, and a music teacher. We used the two lower rooms, one for kitchen and dining room, the other for *family room, reception hall, parlor* and *music room*. During the year, our matriculation went up to seventy-five. We held the first commencement May, 1891, in the dining room of the Girl's Dormitory. This building contained twenty rooms. The last of November, I moved the school into this building and, after the dedication of the building, christened the Institution as "The Kentucky Holiness College." Toward the close of the year, every phase of the work being entirely new, in much perplexity wife and I prayed and planned every feature of the work as rapidly as we could.

During the conference which was held in Lexington, Kentucky, I had an interview with the presiding bishop, in which the plans and the objective of the school were discussed. I asked him if he would appoint me president of this school if the conference so requested. He said, "I could not. I object to the name, for all of our church schools are supposed to be holiness schools." "I was educated," I replied, "in two of them and I never heard the subject mentioned pro or con." I then told him my religious experience saying to him, "Bishop, you know that I know there are but two divine orders of the ministry in the Methodist church, deacons and elders, and that the bishops are elected from the order of elder to the office of bishop, and therefore we be brethren and I have no right as a Christian to discount your experience as a converted man, if you do not profess the blessing of holiness; nor have you as a brother or minister to discount the experience that I received when I obtained the blessing of holiness as a second, distinct work of grace, subsequent to regeneration, which one of your colleagues obligated me to do, when I was received into the full membership of the conference. As to the name 'holiness college,' I am not pleased with that myself, for its objective is to teach every fundamental doctrine of our holy Christianity in connection with the regular college curriculum, laying special emphasis on the Bible, a clear Christian experience, on regeneration and sanctification backed up by holy living. So soon as we are able to pray through we hope to get a less pretentious name for the college."

Toward the close of the year (having written to many of the brethren asking them to suggest a name) I got the name that did appeal to me one

STRUGGLES AND SUCCESSES 111

day while on my knees in prayer. I believe the Lord gave me the name, "Asbury College." I arose from my knees praising God and went to my library and took down McTyeire's History of Methodism to look up some items in the life of Asbury, and particularly his connection with schools. I found in 1790 Bishop Asbury met six other ministers at Masterson Station. He organized the Kentucky Conference and projected Bethel Academy three miles and a half from Wilmore, being the second Methodist school in America, just one hundred years before the time that Asbury College was founded. I felt that this was a providential coincidence, for all who know the history and character of Bishop Asbury, know that he contended earnestly, in common with Mr. Wesley and their co-adjutors, "for the faith which was once delivered to the saints." That is, free salvation to all men and full salvation from all sin, the secret of Asbury College's origin and success.

Asbury's second year:—We closed our first year's work with an interesting commencement, combining literary and musical entertainments with pronounced full salvation work, getting sinners saved and believers sanctified and the fully saved strengthened and edified, which prevailed through the fifteen years of my administration. I thank God the same plan obtains to this day. Those familiar with commencement exercises of schools know that salvation work is no part of the program, but this school was projected with the thought that any pronounced Christian school should begin the year with special emphasis on Christianity and keep that thought daily before the student body, getting people saved and sanctified along with the regular school work through the year, planning, praying and trusting God that the close of the year should have God's seal on the entire commencement program so as to leave on the minds of the students, as they went to their homes, the thought that Christianity is the biggest thing in a college education, remembering that Jesus said, "Seek ye first the kingdom of God and his righteousness and all these things shall be added unto you." Any fair and common-sense interpretation of this statement from the Teacher of all teachers would involve the facts that all things necessary for the welfare and development of the body, mind and soul were contained in the above Scripture and is a good basis or definition of a real Christian education.

We opened our second year September, 1891 with great encouragement, a good student body, with the hearty approval of our constituency and other friends that had been favorably impressed with the class of work that had been done. The old students were happy and courageous and the new ones soon fell into line. The opening day of school, from that on, was a pronounced religious service—a getting acquainted and a good-fellowship day. The first three or four years the outside world and the neighboring institutions of learning in and outside of the churches were not sparing of their unkind, not to say untrue, criticisms. Many of our critics did not credit us as having a college curriculum or competent teaching force. They would say in derision—*"That thing at Wilmore does nothing but cry, and blubber and shout."* On one occasion a prominent layman said to a presiding elder, "Where are we getting most of our preachers that come into conference these days?" "From that thing at Wilmore," he replied. "What kind of men are they?" asked the prominent and wealthy layman. "About as good as we get from anywhere," he answered. "I am in for taking off our hats," said the layman, "and saying hurrah for the thing that gets there."

In one of the first years of the history of the Institution, I was in Lexington and had been out to the lunatic asylum (*Not as an inmate, but visiting a doctor friend of mine.*) Walking down the street, the following interview took place. A pleasant looking gentleman, who was going my way, saluted me saying, "It is a bright morning, sir." I replied, "Quite so, sir." He inquired, "What might be your name?" I answered "It might be Grover Cleveland (Cleveland was President), but it is not." He smiled and said, "What *is* your name?" I told him. He asked me where I was from. I said, "I am a Methodist preacher and from *spots*, but now I chance to be from Wilmore, Kentucky." "Oh", he said, "Wilmore—that is the place where they have that 'sanctified school' and 'holiness church', is it not?"

I answered, "It is." He then said, "Do you ever see any of the people connected with that school?" I replied, "Oh, yes, It is a small place and I see them every day." He said, "I understand that they are a very peculiar people." I answered, *"That is so."* He said, "Do you go to their services and mix up with them?" I answered, "Oh, yes, frequently." "Well, aren't they fanatical on holiness lines? Some people think so. What do you think about it?" "I like them," I answered, "and think they are teaching correctly the Holy Scriptures." He then said, "Are you connected with them in any way?" I answered, "I am the man that started the work there" and with a flushed face and great confusion he said, "I heartily, heartily beg your pardon, sir." I said, "That is perfectly all right, sir." He said, "Excuse me, I go this way," and I thought he was glad to have another way to go. I said, "If you please, sir, I have courteously answered all your questions; will you do me the courtesy to let me tell you what Asbury College stands for?" And I had the blessed privilege for one hour to preach to him Jesus and full salvation. He stood rather nervously, unconsciously kicking the pavement. He interrupted me more than once by saying "I hate to take your precious time." "It is the Lord's time," I replied. He finally said, "Thank you, Mr. Hughes, I can see no objections to your teachings." "There are none," I answered, "we would be pleased to have you visit us at any time, give you a front seat in our exercises, and have you take a meal with us, and give you some red-hot, Kentucky biscuits." With a cordial hand-shake, we bade each other adieu.

The following incident will show how Asbury College, during its early history, was maligned and misrepresented. An enemy of the school wrote an article which was put in one of the Lexington papers, saying, that the President of the college and, of course, the originator of the school, was a follower of Swineforth, who professed to be Jesus Christ, being located at Rockville, Illinois, who erected a throne before which his followers bowed and prayed to him as he professed to be Jesus Christ. I interviewed the editor on the subject and said to him, "I enter my protest against such a statement of my work at Wilmore." He asked me if I didn't teach something along fanatical lines at Wilmore concerning the Holy Scriptures. I replied, "No, sir, in no sense." This interview occurred in his parlor, where a large Bible was lying on the table. I picked up the Bible and said to him, "Major, (for that was his title), what does this expression mean on the back of your Bible?" He replied, "Holy Book." I then asked, "Does the term Bible mean a Holy Book in itself?" He answered, "It does." I replied, "No sir; it does not in itself. It comes from the Greek word, 'Biblos', which means merely a book, neither good nor bad. The word 'Holy' in front of it describes the teachings of the Book, i. e. a book on Holiness. And Asbury College was based as a Christian school on the teachings of the Holy Bible, and in no sense, we insist, is that teaching fanatical." I then sought an interview with the young lady that contributed the article, handed to her by an enemy of the school that wrote it and asked her why she wrote such an article. She said, "I did not write it, but obtained it through a friend and did not know there would be any objection to it." I said to her, "As you are a nice looking young lady and I think your face indicates that you meant nothing vicious, please tell me why you are in this kind of work." She responded, "For a livelihood." I said to her, "I am in the business of helping to educate and prepare for life work worthy young men and women so that they may be prepared for the honorable professions of life; so if you will come down to Asbury College it shall cost you nothing till you get a more honorable position than to be the means or instrument of putting such falsehoods before the public." She saw the force of my sarcasm more than my liberality. With a cordial hand-shake we bade each other adieu.

The above stories are illustrations of the estimate that the public seemed to have had for several years, of Asbury College. But when the college began to send out young men and women as college professors, preachers, missionaries, writers and those who filled other prominent places, other colleges recognized the college and its president in good fellowship. Professor T. W. Shannon was our first graduate. He came to us as a farm boy, having been one year in college, being one of the eleven charter pupils. Those who have heard him and read his books know that he was a strong preacher and

STRUGGLES AND SUCCESSES 117

a national lecturer and writer on the science of eugenics. He was called to lecture to the major part of the schools, great and small, in the United States. He wrote a number of remarkable books on the subject of eugenics. More than a million copies have been sold. As a college student, he was recognized by the faculty and students as a young man of good ability, a strong body, and indomitable energies made him great. Our second graduate was Rev. B. F. Jones, who has made an excellent, and successful pastor, and is now one of the leading presiding elders of his conference. Our third class of graduates contained five excellent young men and women, all of whom have made good. Among them, was Dr. W. L. Clark, who is now the successful pastor of a large church and college at Wilmore, also Business Manager of the College.

I think I am safe in saying that the first five years of Asbury College closed its Experimental Stage, put it on its feet and gave it recognition both in the ecclesiastical and literary circles. I said "Experimental Stage;" I mean that as a Christian Institution, it had already demonstrated its right and place in the Christian college world. It then began its pronounced work on religious and educational lines as a competitor of other schools. It had, I am sure more than its quota of criticism as to its loud profession, as it was doing a work on the religious lines, different from other colleges, not excepting a good per cent of the church schools. I feel absolutely certain that I am correct in saying, with the eye of God on me, from the first day of the school's existence till the last day that it was under my administration, it progressed sanely and religiously, on all educational lines, as hundreds, not to say thousands, will testify. The class of students we turned out during those entire fifteen years are concrete examples of the kind of work that was done. I state this because it has been insinuated by some that the college under my administration did not have a first-class curriculum, did not have a first-class faculty, did not turn out first-class young men and women as preachers, teachers, missionaries and students in general. I do not believe that any college in this country in the first fifteen years of its history did more for the educational and religious world than did Asbury College.

CHAPTER XII.

ASBURY'S CONFLICTS AND CONQUESTS.

Many of the most pious preachers and laymen spoke of the contrast; it often provoked severe criticism, which generally injured their own work and gave Asbury a free advertisement. A minister friend of mine from boyhood, who for many years has been a missionary in Japan, said to me when I started Kingswood College, "That will mean that you have put it on the world map as you have Asbury College." Asbury's constant enlargement as to buildings, grounds, student body and faculty, so soon as it got out, especially among the holiness people, brought students from twenty states of the Union, Canada and some from foreign countries.

The next stage of the College was its internal and continued financial tests. Except the sixteen hundred dollars given in the location of the school, the school had to support itself; as I had no income from a board or any outside friends. I did not feel free at all to ask my friends for financial help as the Institution at the time was my own private property. One man in California wrote me that he and his wife were in delicate health saying that they had made up their minds to donate their home located in the suburbs of Los Angeles, California, asking me to have the deed made according to the laws of Kentucky and send to him and he and his wife would sign and return it to me. I could not conscientiously accept this donation while the school was in my individual name, but I wrote him that the time might be in the not distant future that I would put it into the hands of a board; then his donation would probably be accepted. I had then, and have now, a perfect horror for handling other people's money in its appropriation other than as they directed. I made up my mind in boyhood days that I would always live in sight of where I could pay my honest debts. And no man could say I got money from him, and recklessly spent it on myself or family. When it was known throughout the country that I had never failed to take a student, or a family of boys and girls because they could not pay their tuition, occasionally some friend would send me a donation to aid some special pupil. I feel that I am correct in saying the twenty-five years of my college life, in Asbury and Kingswood Colleges that one thousand dollars would cover all the donations received to assist needy and worthy students. Not only was the school left open to many for their tuition, but for their board, and tuition, their notes being taken. Most of them have been paid, but thousands of dollars are still unpaid, and the indications are most of it will never be paid.

Asbury College, in common with all other Christian schools, with its *failures* and *successes* has had its *external* and *internal foes* and *hindrances*, "fightings without and fears within." No work of God has ever run smoothly all the time in this *sin-cursed* and *largely devil- dominated world*. I learned long ago that a college which had for its objective the special religious training of its students, would not, or could not run without the devil's and his servants' opposition and interference, for they love what God hates and hate what God loves. Satan is not opposed to educational work, but contrariwise, is a strong advocate; for he can carry out his diabolical schemes better through learned than ignorant men. Hence, *an intense full salvation school*, has the hatred of the devil, and godless men and women, in and out of the church, who will give their sympathy, money and patronage to schools that eliminate God and Christianity and will ignore schools that stand for *God* and *righteousness*. Asbury College has not only had her external tests but strong internal trials and temptations. James said, "Count it all joy when you fall into divers temptations." The cause of God as manifested in His church, in the Israelitish, Apostolic, Reformation, Wesleyan and all successive revivals and movements, and men who have "earnestly contended for the faith once delivered to the saints," have all had their internal testings. So Christian educational work is no exception to other phases of the work of God. Asbury and Kingswood Colleges have had their quota of disturbances and tests. Bringing together a faculty and student body from different parts of the country, seeing things from divers viewpoints, teaching them to think and act in harmony with the truth on all political, scientific, philosophical, and religious issues as honest investigators, is no common task.

A full salvation school is more difficult to manage than a non-religious school; for in a distinctive religious school, each student has his mind free from the thraldom of sin. He feels free to do his own thinking on religious lines; the faculty and students constitute a *religious democracy* which is not always easy to harmonize. First, because some will have zeal not according to knowlege, and some will have more knowledge than zeal, and some may have neither zeal nor knowledge, and some may have crept into the faculty or student body for mercenary purposes, e. g., Judas Iscariot sold his Lord for thirty pieces of silver. Also Simon the Sorcerer, who desired to buy the gift of the Holy Ghost. If Jesus, in selecting twelve men for his apostolic council, should have one false counsellor, and an *early aspostolic evangelist should have one false convert in a pentecostal revival,* no church or institution of learning conducted by human skill may expect to be fully exempted from the possibility of similar experiences.

During my administration I saw Asbury College close three years of what I regarded as among its most successful years, in great perplexity and confusion despite all my efforts to keep it in perfect harmony with God and His truth. After all, thank God, it always closed with divine approval and with clearcut and full salvation work. All I could do each year was to trust God to bring human confusion into order and future prosperity. And this He always did by the opening of the next session. And I see now, as never before, the imperative need of wide awake, common sense religious school work, even stronger than I did in my earlier days, to combat our modern so-called education where evolution and destructive criticism are so dogmatically and daringly emphasized by the egotistical and narrow scholars who have denied all the fundamental teachings of the Holy Scriptures. They take the supernatural out of God and Christianity, deify man, humanize God and minify sin. All the advocates of Modernism make, as the basis of their investigation, physical science which is the lowest of the sciences known to man—physical, mental and theological. With all their pretended scholarship they bring all their psychological and theological studies to the basis of the laws of matter, which is inexcusable among all correct thinkers. But the most tremendous mistake they make is a failure to discover that the Bible and Christianity can only be discerned with spiritual eyes, "But the natural man receives not the things of the Spirit of God; for they are *foolishness* unto him; neither can he know them, because they are spiritually discerned." The *Bible* is *primarily* a *spiritual* book, and cannot be understood, except through men who have a spiritual insight into God. Hence, the mistake the so-called scientists are making, when they try to understand the Scriptures through mere mental processes. All Christian scholarship agrees that God's universe is governed by laws in perfect harmony with each other, never blending; but each line of law operating in its particular sphere. Hence, there can be no conflict. For He who made the laws of nature to operate the physical sphere, made mental laws to operate the intellectual sphere, and spiritual laws to operate the spiritual sphere. Therefore, those who teach the discrepancy between science and the Bible have an absolute misconception of both science and the Bible. Yet a large per cent of our schools are dominated with this false and *soul destroying heresy*, so-called science. Hence, the absolute need of schools that teach and constantly emphasize the fundamentals of the Holy Scriptures as to the character of God, His creating and superintending work in the redemption of all men from all sin, and teaching man his origin, duty and destiny.

Asbury College was owned and conducted as an individual, independent and interdenominational institution with no financial backing at all. But from the beginning it grew rapidly, but became such a personal burden to bear alone, after much thought and prayer I concluded to put it into a corporation to be managed by a Board, of which I was to be exofficio chairman as its president. This was to relieve me of some of my responsibilities and put the college on a basis that it would not depend for its existence on any one individual, and it would then be in a condition to appeal to the holiness people for general assistance and its enlargement and permanency so that its future success might be assured. I therefore sold it on the following conditions; that I was to remain its president so long as I felt the

Lord led in that direction. The board estimated the property at forty thousand dollars and I agreed to take thirty thousand and donate five thousand of that to the college and they were to pay me fifteen thousand dollars in cash or its equivalent and the remainder at their convenience so long as I remained its president. And, as its president, when the debt was fully met I was to donate the last thousand dollars. The property was as follows: Fourteen and one quarter acres of land; a large brick administration building with a chapel up stairs having seating capacity for nine hundred people, one recitation room and a large museum. Seven large recitation rooms down stairs with a spacious hall, the building being heated with furnaces; three frame dormitories for boys containing forty rooms; two dormitories for girls containing thirty rooms; president's cottage and primary, which meant a donation by myself, according to the estimate made by the board, of sixteen thousand dollars, which I gladly invested in order to insure permanency to the institution, as I saw a great possible future for it, if it was rightly conducted.

The question arises as to how I came to change my relation to Asbury College when I sold the Institution to the Board with the specific understanding that I was to remain the president as long as the Lord directed. This *proviso* was not unreasonable in view of the fact that I was practically giving sixteen thousand dollars to the Institution. Being ex-officio Chairman of the Board I was asked by the Vice President to call the Board together. There was just a quorum including myself. I had no idea what the call was, and after answering a certain line of questions concerning the school was asked to retire. Of course I did not understand the significance of it. In the meantime a phone message came to me from a man in Texas informing the Board that he would take the position offered him. I immediately went back to the Board and asked what this message meant. I learned that the Board was planning to make a change in the Presidency, which was done illegally because there was not a quorum when I was absent. The legality and constitutionality of the procedure might have been challenged, but I was so dazed and dumfounded, perplexed and grieved that I left and let them take their course. Thus ended my presidency of Asbury College.

My first successor was Dr. B. F. Haynes of Nashville, Tennessee, a scholarly Christian gentleman, who did his best to make a success of the school. He was employed by the Board to run the Institution for five years. For some reason or other he resigned after three years. His successor was Dr. Newton Wray, who was Dean but acted as President for one year. Next in order was Dr. Aaron S. Watkins, prominent in prohibition work, who served as president of the Institution for one year. In the meantime two main buildings were burned. The school gradually degenerated to such an extent that the

Chairman of the Board at the time said to me: "I can assure you that the Board would do anything in its power to get you back as president, provided you would consider it." I answered that I could not under any circumstances consider it, as I was president of Kingswood College, and felt as far as I knew that I would spend the rest of my college days there.

These incidents and events are recited, not for my own vindication, but in the interest of the facts in the case which form one of the main links in the historical chain of the Institution.

CHAPTER XIII.

TRIP TO PALESTINE

All my student life I had a great longing to see the land of the Bible. On June 1st, 1905, at the close of my last year as president of Asbury College, I bade my friends adieu, kissed my wife and children goodbye and took the morning train for Cincinnati. When I looked toward my precious family and my friends and dear old Asbury, my heart felt like it would almost break within me.

In my company were two of my old students, C. A. and H. W. Bromley; and I am persuaded that no man ever went to Palestine with two companions who were cleaner in life and language and with whom he could have more delightful fellowship. By the time we were half way to Cincinnati, in order to dispel the homesickness (of both them and myself,) we took our eyes off the home environments, as far possible, centered them on our objective, and taking new courage turned our thoughts toward the Holy Land.

On reaching Cincinnati we bought our traveling checks and started for New York. We landed there Friday, June 2nd, got our passes endorsed and spent the night at Barraccah Home with my good friend, Dr. A. B. Simpson, the projector of that great Alliance Missionary Movement. It had been my privilege some years before to spend ten days with him,

ASBURY COLLEGE ADMINISTRATION BUILDING.

with his work and workers; and it gives me pleasure to say I was never with a man, or even in a place, where I was more conscious of the presence of God than I was when I was with this sainted man, his co-workers and student body. The Doctor and his work stood for the four-fold Gospel: regeneration, the baptism of the Holy Ghost, divine healing, and the second coming of Christ. It was an epoch in my life to be associated with those holy, sane, God-filled and God-led people. The night we were there he preached on Divine healing, and followed the sermon with an anointing service. Upon the leader and his work I felt the conscious presence and approval of God, so unlike my visit to Alexander Dowie. The week I spent with Mr. Dowie and his work I felt equally conscious that neither Mr. Dowie nor his workers had the divine approval; for neither regeneration, nor the baptism of the Holy Spirit was emphasized by Mr. Dowie, nor was it sought by the people. The healing of the body received all the emphasis.

Saturday morning, June 3rd, about 10:00 o'clock we first looked upon the Princess Irene, the steamer which was to take us on our first ocean voyage. A great multitude had gathered on the beach to bid their friends goodbye. One of my former teachers, Miss Reeves, then living in New York, and B. L. Sarmast, one of my old students, enroute to Oroomia, Persia, as a missionary to his own people, were the only two familiar faces in that great company to bid us goodbye. The gang plank was taken in at

11:00 o'clock, the signal given, and our first ocean voyage began. We sailed out of New York Bay by the Goddess of Liberty, praying and hoping for a safe and enjoyable voyage. Things seemed to be in a measure normal until we lost sight of the last tree top; then nothing was in sight but the sky above, the water beneath, and the Princess Irene loaded with commercial and human freight. In a moment the normal beginning was changed into the abnormal. The good ship seemed to take on new courage and seemingly went down at least twenty feet. Then we and other new sailors began to walk and stagger like drunken men, stepping up when the ship went down and stepping down when the ship went up. A ship has three distinct movements; back and forth, the long way from east to west and the short way from north to south; and the third movement was a churning process that stirred the stomach and its contents, which constitutes what is known as sea sickness. However, our fourteen days' voyage to Naples, Italy, was very pleasant. Only one day of real sea-sickness to most of the tourists. Our fifth day out we spent much of our time on deck, bathing in the beautiful sunshine and ocean breeze, and discovered land ahead, which was always a welcome sight. It was a great monotony in seeing only water beneath and sky above; so all passengers were out looking at what proved to be the Azores Islands, and exquisite mountain scenery. Their little vegetable farms looked like a crazy quilt. The Portugese, the inhabitants of these Islands, have small bits of land, which they so thoroughly cultivate to make a living.

We had our letters prepared for our Kentucky wives, telling them we were yet alive, and in a good measure sober. These we dropped into a box and the box was dropped into the ocean as we sailed by the Islands. By this time I began to have some appreciation of an ocean voyage that had been described to me by friends who had had like experiences. One of my friends, Col. T. B. Demaree, gave me the following story. He said in the midst of a storm most all on board were sick, but he had the good fortune not to be sick. He said he went to an old lady, who, like himself, had escaped the sea sickness, and an old gentleman, sitting by her was quite sick, and had laid his head on her shoulder. He said, I remarked to her, "I am sorry to see your husband so sick," and she replied, "husband, nothing, I never saw this man before." The Colonel's explanation was that in case of sea sickness some things were permissible that were not allowable under ordinary circumstances. He also gave me another story. He said a bride and groom were spending their honeymoon on an ocean voyage, and the bride was standing the voyage splendidly, but the groom had a good case of sea sickness, and they were standing on deck after their seven o'clock meal. (For they have from seven to nine lunches a day, and you are left to your own option as to how many of them you partake of.) The groom was disposing of his evening meal into the mighty deep, and his bride came up and said, "My dear, I am so sorry to see you so sick." For the present he had neither the time nor the strength to respond. She then tried to divert his attention from himself by saying, "Is the moon up?" He responded with unusual emphasis, "If it went down it is up, for everything that went down has come up."

From the Azores Islands we sailed six days out of sight of land, then through our field glasses we again discovered land, which proved to be Gibraltar, on which we spent several hours looking through the barracks of the English boys, and viewing their cannon, which projected through the rock of Gibraltar, facing the straits to the Mediterranean, and No Man's Land, a little strip of land owned by no government, and, of course controlled by no government. It was once a place of refuge for outlaws of all nations.

In three days after leaving Gibraltar we reached Naples, in southern Italy, a city of 350,000 people. This is the largest city in Italy, and said to be on one of the prettiest bays in the world. The city is built in a half moon shape on the plan of an amphitheatre. Many things of historic character claimed the attention of the tourists. Among them were the following: the Tomb of Virgil, the magnificent museum, Vesuvius and the cities of Pompeii and Herculaneum, located about ten miles from the city of Naples. From the veranda of our hotel, that opened out on the bay, we had a fine view of Vesuvius, which was quite active at that time. In addition to the smoke that continually ascended from the crater, a great fissure said to be about 200 feet, had been made on the side of the volcano, which was unceasingly emitting lava, making one of the most spectacular scenes I ever saw. We were not allowed to visit the crater as the authorities, on account of its activity, had forbidden any one to go to its top.

We next visited the great museum. It is worth any one's while when in Naples to spend some time in this museum, especially if they have an artistic taste. Uufortunately I could not fully appreciate the great museums I have visited in different countries, and cannot describe them as an artist can; but I shall always appreciate my contact with them and with the artists that could appreciate them. After a short visit to the tomb of Virgil, with many less points of interest, we took ship for Port Said, Egypt, a town at the mouth of the Suez Canal, but of no special notoriety, except it is in the historic land of Egypt.

The most remarkable thing to me was two meals I ordered while in the city of Port Said, Egypt, neither of which I could eat; first, because of their meats and most everything else. It seemed to me they were akin to Polk Miller's cheese. Some of my readers will remember Polk Miller, the Virginia plantation negro imitator. Once upon a time Mr. Miller had a banquet prepared for his literary friends. When the colored man told him everything was in readiness, he invited his guests to the table. After they had begun their feast he called the colored man to him, and said, "Sam, what did you do with the Limberger cheese?" Sam replied, in an undertone, "Boss, sho' ez ye bo'n, dey have been on hand too long." All through that country they had on the table a cheese they called "Gongozola" which was surely a cousin to the Limberger. I aimed to sit as far from it as I could. One day a Major of the Salvation Army in London, who had been traveling with me for several days, sat at a hotel table with me at Port Said, and they put the cheese next to me. I said "Major, in the name of common sense and humanity, take that thing from under my nose." He laughed and said, "Do you know what kind of meat you are eating?" I said, "No, I am glad I have eaten none as yet." He said "That's horse." If you could see the usual work horse about the time he is superannuated and mysteriously transformed into beefsteak you would not criticise me for excusing myself from the Major, and, with a nauseated and empty stomach, paying the proprietor and taking a little walk and another look at the Mediterranean Sea.

Having spent parts of two days and one night at Port Said we took train 150 miles across the desert into the Delta and to Cairo, now the capital and the largest city in Egypt. We crossed the land of Goshen, and, across the route that the Israelites traveled in their exit out of Egypt, across the Red Sea and into the wilderness. We spent a number of days in Cairo and its environs. It is almost exclusively a Mohammedan city. They claim to have

14,000 boy students in one school, sitting on the floor, memorizing and studying the Koran, (the Mohammedan Bible.) I say boys, because the girls are supposed to have no souls and do not need to study their holy book. We visited their great Museum which contained many curiosities, particularly the mummy of Ramases the Second, who led his army and was supposed to be drowned in the Red Sea while pursuing the children of Israel. The last day I was in this building I spent most of the time alone, which is by far the best way for a careful investigation in such places.

Next, we visited Cheops, the greatest of the pyramids and also the burial place of many of their noted dead. The historian Myers gives the following description of this Pyramid: "From a base covering thirteen acres to a height of 450 feet, according to Herodotus, Cheops employed one hundred thousand men for twenty years in its erection." I climbed the pyramid to its summit without the assistance of the pestilential beggars, two of whom generally aid the tourists both up and down, one in front hold of the tourists hands pulling, and the other behind, with his hands just above the tourists hips pushing. As I expected to go up and down it but one time I shook my head and said, "No." They persisted as I climbed but finally got discouraged and said, "America, he go, he go." When standing on the top with my fellow tourists, seeing in the clear air in every direction, possibly from forty to sixty miles, one of the party quoted that noted statement of Bonaparte to his soldiers: "Men, forty centuries are looking down upon you. Let each man do his best."

My fellow tourists and I had our photographs taken under that broiling Egyptian sun, and one of those chronic beggars who had followed us up to the pyramid, looked at me, holding out his hand and asked, "Are you worth $5,000,000?" I said, "No." He finally brought it down to $1,000,000 as I continued to say no. He looked at me as if he felt I was not telling the truth, coming that far and not being a millionaire. I then pointed to myself and fellow tourists and said: "Poor preachers, poor preachers, preach Jesus, not much money, not much money." After a wearisome day, having gone to the hotel, gotten a bath and supper, one of my fellow tourists and I went across to a plaza (park), where a brass band was playing. I looked at the moon with her familiar face and into the starry heavens and thought of my old Kentucky home and precious family. While thus musing, I had a little touch of homesickness, and at this opportune moment the band played "Old Kentucky Home." All the patriotism I had in me rushed to the front, and I was tempted to rise and throw my hat in the air and hurrah for Kentucky, and the Stars and Stripes.

I preached one night to the English soldier boys in the army of Occupation. We next returned to Port Said where we took ship for Palestine, which we ought to have reached in fifteen hours but having a case of the Black Plague on ship we passed by Joppa and went to northern Syria to Beirut where we were in quarantine thirty-five hours. Not being permitted to go to the shore we got to see the town only from the ship. In the morning about 8:00 o'clock, before many of the tourists were out on the deck, they had what they called ship practice, creating quite a commotion. They were taking down the small life boats which were used in the case of fire or leakage of the ship, or for any other occurrence that would jeopardize the life of the passengers. They did it so enthusiastically that I thought the ship was on fire and started to tell my fellow tourists who were still in their room. I said to several of the men, "What is the matter, what is the matter?" They shook their heads and went on. I grabbed one of them and held him and said, "What is the matter here?" His answer was, "Practice."

At the expiration of thirty-five hours, sailing along the coast of Syria we passed the little towns of Tyre and Sidon at night when we could see but little of them. We saw land next morning for several hours before we reached the little town of Java (Joppa) about eleven o'clock. We were held there for some time in quarantine. At most of the seaports the ships have to cast anchor some distance from the beach, and the passengers are transferred to the beach in small boats called tenders, meaning oar boats. On landing, of all the sights and confusion I have ever witnessed was among those small boatmen, pulling at each passenger, talking in their various unknown tongues, in their varied modes of dress. When once seen it will never be forgotten.

This is said to be the most dangerous seaport in the world. We got into a little boat, wiggling around among other similar boats, with all the boatmen hollowing and apparently abusing each other. We were taken to shore in a zigzag way between the projecting rocks on either side and put our feet for the first time on Syrian soil at the little historic town of Joppa.

We first visited the building that was supposed to be the house on which Peter was praying when God gave him the vision which convinced him that God meant the gospel for the Gentiles as well as the Jews. It is a small building made of limestone, and probably it is the identical building that the Bible mentions. We then visited, in the suburbs of the town, the home of Dorcas, who in answer to Peter's prayers, was raised from the dead. These two visits introduced us to the sacred history and supernatural works of Jesus and His disciples. We then boarded a train for Jerusalem, forty miles distant. Passing first through the valley of Sharon (about 12 miles in width) through beautiful groves, we struck the mountain scenery, and following a zigzag road mostly in the valley we reached the depot of the city of Jerusalem, situated on Mount Zion and Moriah about a half mile away, near six o'clock, Saturday afternoon.

When I left my friend, Dr. A. B. Simpson, in New York, he promised me he would write his missionaries in Jerusalem and have them meet us at the depot and take us to Jerusalem and give us some aid in seeing the city. I had notified them from Joppa that we would be on the next train. They gave us a cordial reception and took us in their carriage up to the gate of the City, and showed us many kindnesses. I preached one Sunday night in their mission. It was my first and only sermon through an interpreter. We got out of the carriage at the gate of the City took our hats off, and entered the sacred City with our mind crowded with sacred memories of "The Man of Galilee," His life, work, death and ascension to Glory. We first inquired for a hotel where they both talked and cooked somewhat on the American style; for our bill-of-fare in Southern Italy, and on the Mediterranean Sea, and in Egypt had been so un-American that our stomachs had made a strike, and we had to make some compromise or they would quit their job. The hotel chanced to be run by people from England. It was also the home of our American Consul and his wife, who had been there for years. They were originally from the State of Wisconsin. When they heard that some Americans had arrived they came down to see us. Having been introduced there sprang up a fellow feeling between us at once. His wife asked if we were going to put up at this hotel. I answered: "That depends on the service of the culinary department, whether or not they will give us food prepared somewhat on American style, for we cannot stand much longer the food we have been getting for the past several weeks." She replied, "We will help to look after that matter," which she did nobly. I shall always regard it as one of the most delightful experiences of good fellowship in my life. They were a very superior couple, and did all in their power to make our trip both pleasant and profitable. They seemed to enjoy our party, for we made ourselves as agreeable as possible, answering such questions about the States as we were capable of answering.

After getting located in our rooms, and having a good bath and a sure enough American prepared supper, we took a little stroll out into the city. Returning to our hotel and getting a splendid night's rest, about four o'clock next morning, I was awakened by a peculiar, distressing noise. I ran to my veranda which faced the main street of the city, and the noise seemed to be so distressing that I thought some one was being murdered, but it was explained to me later that it was the Mohammedan call for prayer. From the cupola of the mosque (church) this call is made five times a day. Every true Mohammedan wherever he chances to be, turns his face toward Mecca and either stands or falls prostrate and prays.

I arranged my toilet at once, and with Bible in hand started for the Mount of Olives, by the way of the Eastern Gate. The streets are so constructed, and seemed to run into each other and run out where they ought not, that I got so confused about how to find the Gate, that I had to ask a Franciscan Monk the way to Mount Olivet. I had met his kind before, dressed in brown, hair shaved off the top of his head, covered with a little brown cap. He understood only "Mount Olivet." The way I made him understand was by my vigorous gyrations. He motioned to me to follow him. By so doing I soon saw the Eastern Gate, and the dear old Kentucky sun coming up over Mount Olivet, shining into the Kidron Valley, and over the historic city. His face was so homelike and friendly, compared with my other environments, that I took courage and pursued my morning visit. Going down to the Kidron Valley that separates the city from the Mount of Olives, taking in the Garden of Gethsemane, so thrilled with the sight of these historic places I became oblivious, for the time of the passersby, and was shocked tremendously by three women lepers who rose up near me with plaintive cries, "Bacshesh Bacshesh." Taking in the situation I walked around these afflicted beggars and on to the Garden of Gethsemane.

I had studied carefully the location of this Garden before going to that country, and knew that it was on the western side of the Mount of Olives. While viewing this sacred historical spot, my heart was profoundly impressed, as my imagination reproduced the scenes that occurred there two thousand years ago, when the "Man of Galilee" went before the Heavenly Father in agonizing prayer saying: "If it be possible let this cup pass from me; nevertheless not my will but thine be done." I visited this Garden every morning while I was in Jerusalem, reading some portion of the Scriptures bearing on the experience of our Lord in those tragic moments. I have never felt worthy to say that I had been put to a Gethsemane test, similar to my Lord. However, I was at that time undergoing the severest test of my life, with a perplexed head and a heart as heavy as lead. I had hoped when I reached this historic spot that there would be a breaking up of my emotional nature, and that I might have a hearty cry which would give vent to my pent-up sorrows. I implored the Lord for such an experience, but in His wisdom He withheld what my sad heart hungered for. I said with all the faith and courage I could command, "Father, not my will but thine be done." I continued my Sunday morning trip to the top of the Mount of Olives, where I had a conspicious view of the Kidron Valley and the City of Jerusalem.

The old city proper, inside the wall, contained sixty thousand people. There were forty nationalities speaking forty languages or dialects. I have no language to express the overwhelming awe that possessed my soul, when I realized that I sat on the spot where my Lord stood and wept over its wickedness two thousand years ago, saying, "Oh Jerusalem! Jerusalem! how oft would I have gathered thee under my wings as a hen doth her chickens, and ye would not." Sitting on a pile of rock I read the Sermon on the Mount, and thought of what Jesus said concerning the coming destruction of this city, when some of its inhabitants assured Him that it was so protected by its high walls that it would stand the tests of its enemies. He replied, "Not one stone shall rest upon another," which prophecy was fulfilled under Titus, the Roman general, in about a half a century later.

By this time the church bells were ringing, and, as I looked upon the desolation of the country surrounding the city, and had begun to see the conglomerate condition of the religions of the city, I felt those bells represented effete religions that were perpetuated by hatred toward each other, leaving out the God who made and redeemed them. I read the thirteenth chapter of first Corinthians, feeling in my heart that those confused forms of religion were fully described in this chapter, and particularly in the first verse: "Though I speak with the tongues of men and angels and have not charity (love), I am become as sounding brass or a tinkling cymbal."

I am sure I had a fair estimate of the degenerated conditions of this city, which had had more light in its history than any other city in the world. Patriarchs, Prophets, Christ and His apostles, all filled with God, once spake there as the Spirit gave them utterance; but this marvelous concentration of light had been rejected, and the result was dense darkness. Confusion of thought, confusion of language, confusion of standards of teaching and right living had overwhelmed that God-forsaking and God-forsaken people for twenty centuries, making it one of the most difficult cities and countries in the world to reach with our holy Christianity. It is a literal fulfillment of the prophecies of the Old

Testament, of Jesus and the writers of the New Testament. No wonder that the Immaculate Teacher, on his way from Pilate's judgment hall to Calvary's rugged brow, when his disciples were weeping over the world's greatest tragedy just ahead of them, said, "Weep not for me, but for yourselves and your children." No doubt his own disciples, who saw Him nailed to the cross, and those who helped to nail Him there, saw the significance of the above words, when the city was surrounded with the Roman soldiers, and the inhabitants within the walls died through starvation by the thousands, and mothers ate their own offspring; and the end is not yet.

I visited what is known as the Jewish wailing place outside of the Southern Gate of the City, where daily the old and young among the Jews were reading the Old Testament Scriptures, weeping, wailing, and crying to God, the Father of Abraham, Isaac and Jacob to restore unto them the Kingdom of Israel, and bring to them their promised Messiah, whose truth, in their blindness, they had rejected two thousand years ago. For Jesus had said to their fathers, and through the Old Testament Scriptures, "Search these scriptures, for in them ye think ye have eternal life, and they are they which testify of me;" but their fathers said, "Away with Him, away with Him." And for two thousand years the rejecting Jews, following in the footsteps of their fathers, are still saying, "away with Him" whose name is known to the ends of the earth as the Maker and Redeemer of all men, as the only hope of a lost world, as the only name given among men whereby man can be saved. Away with the thought that honest rejecting Jews or the Paganistic world, can be saved without Jesus Christ, who lighteth every man that cometh into the world.

In conversation with a great preacher and teacher, a while ago, we were discussing a man who denied the Divinity of Christ and who has done more, both by preaching and writing, than any other man in America to spread the heresy of Unitarianism which, in my judgment, is the basis of modern evolution and Destructive Criticism. When I asked him what was the hope of this man's future, he said, "I would not say of him what a Methodist preacher said to me once, namely, that he had been in Hell burning ever since he died." I said to the doctor, "I feel sure he has been in Hell burning or in Heaven rejoicing; for there are but two final destinies for man; and I am forced to the conclusion, that as he rejected the Divinity of Christ, that he could not be in Heaven shouting; for Jesus is the only name whereby man can be saved." He then replied, "I leave him in the hands of a merciful God." I thought then, and still think, that the devil, once an Angel of Light, was left in the hands of a meciful God, but is now the Arch-enemy of God and man, the prince of Demons. I also met another great preacher, who thought it might be possible for the now Christ-rejecting Jews to be saved.

Leaving my seat on the Mount of Olives, retracing my steps by the way of Gethsemane back to the Eastern Gate of the City, again coming in contact with the three mentioned lepers, I threw each of them a small piece of money; and, getting a careful view of these dreadful sufferers I found their feet and hands were almost entirely destroyed. I feel I am correct in saying, by the time I entered the Gate, that I saw about one hundred similarly afflicted. Then, with a heavy heart and perplexed head I returned to my hotel near the West Gate, went to my room and prayed God to take the burden of these afflicted people off my mind, and give me a clear mind and cheerful heart so that I might accurately behold the City that I had longed all my student life to see. God answered my prayer, and I was permitted to put in my best energies in taking in the City and its environments during the next ten days.

The following morning, after breakfast, I and my fellow tourists visited the Holy Sepulcher. It was a large, rotund building, which had four small chapels opening into it, namely, the Roman Catholic, Greek Catholic, Armenian Catholic and Copt Catholic, all branches of the general Catholic Church and bitter enemies of each other. They all held services at the same time, which produced confusion doubly confounded, and which impressed the tourists more as the service of the devil than of God. Often at their great feasts their antagonism results in murder; hence, the Turkish soldiers are there to keep order. They have inside the Rotunda two small rooms not joined together. One is called the room of the Holy Sepulcher containing the Sarcophagus of the supposed body of Jesus. The worshipers are constantly entering that room and kissing the Sarcophagus. The other room is called the Angels room where the Greek Catholics, in their annual feast are taught that they receive holy fire from Heaven through an aperture in the wall of the room. Thousands of worshipers come thousands of miles with torches in hand to be lighted in the Holy Fire, which they believe will burn up sin. There is one called a Patriarch concealed in that room, and, when the door of the Rotunda is open the people press for life to that hole in the wall; and the Patriarch inside removes the covering, and the fire comes out of the aperture. Those nearest light their torches, and those who cannot get near light their torches from the others, and soon each one's torch is lighted. Confusion and torture which the crowd undergoes must be similar to that of lost souls in perdition. Each one applies the torch to himself on different parts of the body, supposing that he has rid himself of sin. I asked my guide why this farce was not explained to the people by their leaders and an end put to it. He said, "That question had often been asked the Patriarch, and his reply was, 'If it was explained as a sham the church would believe all of its customs were sham.'"

CHAPTER XIV.

JERUSALEM AND ITS ENVIRONS.

The first day of July, 1905, at about six o'clock in the afternoon, we entered Jerusalem, or the Holy City, with our heads uncovered. Through a thirty feet opening in the west wall south of the Java Gate, that was made by the Sultan of Turkey in honor of the Emperor of Germany, who had promised to visit his country. This is the broadest street in the city. The usual streets are from eight to eleven feet. The streets are of solid limestone, and the buildings are of the same material. On entering this city of the world's most sacred memories, the heart feels peculiarly solemn, feeling that probably they are walking in the footsteps of the patriarchs, prophets, and Jesus of Nazareth, and His disciples. As soon as we entered the gate we came to a splendid hotel, run by an English firm, where, fortunately, we found our consul and his excellent wife, the Spanish consul and other dignitaries here located. While talking to the landlord and the landlady, telling them of our trip over Italy, Mediterranean Sea to Egypt, where the water and food were to us Americans almost unendurable, our plaintive cry was "Can you give us some food and water on the order of the Americans'?" The consul and his wife hearing our story, assured us that if we would remain there and talk to them about America, they would see that our request was

JERUSALEM AND ITS ENVIRONS 149

granted, and would be glad to do anything in their power to put us in possession of such facts as we desired in Jerusalem, its immediate environs, and throughout the country of Palestine. We had splendid fellowship together with this excellent couple, also the Spanish consul and other dignitaries, and excellent service given us by the culinary department. And our twelve days spent in Jerusalem as headquarters, left the most delightful memories that we shall not soon forget. After we had been there a number of days, and, taken in the situation in some measure, I said to our consul "These pestiferous flies are the most persistent things I have ever had to contend with, for they take their position with a seeming determination never to retire until they are forced to." The Spanish consul, a very companionable young gentleman, noted for his real wit and fun, said, "Mr. Hughes, the Syrian fly is as much surprised at you nervous Americans as you are of them. For they have been in the habit of taking their positions undisturbed." Which I had seen in numerous cases around the eyes and mouths of many of its inhabitants who did not seem to be disturbed by them at all.

We attended the Alliance Mission in that city that night, the one projected by that wonderful man, A. B. Simpson, of New York. We found his missionaries there pious, Spirit-filled people. Here I had my first and only opportunity to preach the gospel through an interpreter. On Monday morning quite early we started for Bethlehem and Hebron. The first six miles south of Jerusalem, the cleanest town, of ten thousand inhabitants that we saw in the Holy Land. Of course, we found out the best we could through its inhabitants and our guide the place where Jesus was born and laid in a manger. There, as everywhere else in a city, we heard many foolish traditions, that doubtless had been repeated through the centuries as to the identical spot of his birth. But of one thing we were assured, it was the town in which He was born and it was a sacred and wonderful privilege that most persons are denied. We took our dinner at Hebron, the Cave of Macpelah that contains the sacred dust of Abraham, Sarah, Isaac, Rebekah, Jacob and Leah (for Rachel had been buried six miles south of Jerusalem, whose grave we visited.) Our guide pointed out to us while we were eating our dinner a clump of trees, pehaps a mile away, saying that that was the spot where Abraham lived when God sent angels to notify him of the destruction of Sodom and Gomorrah. On our return trip we took in Solomon's three great pools and fragments of the Aqueduct built of stone in which the water was taken to supply Jerusalem.

Next morning we started for the river Jordan and the Red Sea. We visited the spring near the ruins of Jericho where Elisha made the bitter water sweet. We spent the night in an unoccupied hotel. About sixty to one hundred yards from this hotel there was a caravan of Arabs camping who were enroute to Jerusalem with their wheat from the land of Moab. I had been warned by our consul not to make this trip without a soldier guard of twelve men. A Methodist preacher, formerly from Georgia said to me, "I'll take you for the pleasure. I'm not afraid if you are not." We were not disturbed until the guide called us next morning at six. We ate our breakfast and started for the river Jordan which was several miles away. We bathed in this historic river and swam across to the land of Moab. We also bathed that day in the Dead Sea. The Dead Sea was the most attractive water in which I had ever bathed. All you have to do there is to keep your feet off the bottom and it will float you. It is as clear as crystal notwithstanding that the muddy, crooked Jordan empties into it. The Dead Sea is forty miles long and twelve miles wide. Its outlet, if any, is unknown.

There are macadamized roads made of limestone, the same as our limestone in Kentucky, leading twenty miles to Hebron, twenty miles to the river Jordan, forty miles to Joppa and fifty miles to the Mediterranean Sea at Keifer to the Sea of Galilee.

While we were bathing in the Dead Sea a squad of Turkish soldiers came and demanded from us $2.50 each. I saw my guide was having trouble with them and I asked him what they were talking about, and he told me what they demanded. When he agreed to take me to the Dead Sea I agreed to stand by him at any cost, saying that I was not afraid to go without a soldier guard. I told him to tell them that we belonged to Uncle Sam and lived under the Stars and Stripes. They ceased at once to discuss the matter and retired.

On our return trip to Jerusalem we stopped at what is known as a Kahm, a country hotel where the man was taken by the good Samaritan that fell among the thieves. Men are often held up at that point or near there and robbed. We escaped any other trouble.

We saw the home of Mary, Martha and Lazarus, at the southeastern corner of the Mount of Olives, at the little town of Bethany, where, as all Bible students will remember, Jesus frequently went for retirement after His strenuous days at Jerusalem. We then visited the Mount of Olives, which is the highest mountain in that part of the country. Standing upon its top you can look over the walls of the city and see the entire city of Jerusalem. Passing Gethsemane at the west side of the Mount of Olives, thence across the city to the west gate to the valley of Gihon. Following that valley some distance where it joins the valley of Kedron, constitutiting the valley of Jehosaphat or Hinnom, we came to David's threshing floor, where we saw them threshing out wheat in the old fashioned way throwing their wheat and chaff into the air and the wind driving the chaff away.

Going up the Mount of Olives, astride a small Syrian donkey, we dismounted to cut off some olive branches as souvenirs to bring to our Kentucky homes, a Syrian woman ran up to us and demanded *"Bacshesh."* As neither understood the other's language, and of course, I did not know how to reply to her, I hurriedly mounted my donkey, which I had named Jack. I struck him a pretty hard stroke and told him to move up rapidly. He did so, giving one of the most unearthly yells that I ever heard come from the throat of a donkey. I said to him, "Thank you, Jack. I could not answer that woman so as to be understood, but I am sure that she understood you perfectly."

I said to a man in the mosque of Omah, "Allah (God) Jesus Christ?" He said, "No. Allah, Mohammed. Jesus Christ, prophet, good man. Mohammed, greater prophet." I saw a large stone weighing tens of thousands of tons in the mosque from which their guide told me Mohammed ascended to heaven, leaving the print of his foot on the stone, and the print of Gabriel's hand. They further teach in the Koran that Gabriel went with Mohammed to the third heaven and the way became so rugged that Mohammed went the rest of the way to the seventh heaven, the throne of God, and received from God the Koran (the Mohammedan Bible). In my judgment it is the most thorough jargon of nonsense I have read. It also teaches the only hope that women have for future life is being a faithful wife among possibly a half dozen other wives, that have served a husband faithfully here and he will take them into his heaven, which is one of impurity, to serve him through all eternity. God pity the day when that type of religion shall further dominate the world.

There are three prevailing religions in Palestine: The Moslem, Jew and Christian, the latter mostly Catholic. They have three sabbaths, with no sabbath in fact. That is, the Mohammedan keeps Friday, and of course the Jew and Christian pay no attention to that day. The Jew keeps Saturday and the Mohammedan and Christian do not pay that day any attention. The Christian keeps the first day of the week and the Jew and Mohammedan having had their sabbaths, pay no attention to that day. So of course, to a tourist, every day in Jerusalem seems to be the same.

The Jewish wailing place, outside the wall of Jerusalem near the south Gate of the city, indicates more zeal and earnestness than any service that I saw in that country. Old men stand in this wailing place reading earnestly their Bibles or praying at the top of their voices. Some younger men and women are crying at the top of theirs, but these do not, however, seem to be much in earnest. They are said to be paid mourners, being paid by the rich Jews of this country to do their wailing for them.

After studying these religions, seeing the bitter antagonism between them, and the lifelessness of the little Protestantism, except the missions, my heart was grieved beyond expression over the horrible religious status of that historic and sacred city, which should provoke any earnest Christian heart to lament over the lamentable condition of dear old Palestine. My constant heart cry while viewing these situations was, "Lord, deliver this

JERUSALEM AND ITS ENVIRONS 155

country from the Moslem misrule." The day that General Allenby, with his staff and soldiers, with heads bare, entered the west gate and the news was flashed over the wires, was one of the happiest days of my life, for I saw for the first time any real hope for the possible recovery of that country from the most misgoverned people in the world.

I was told by a minister of the gospel, coming to me third-handed from General Allenby, that the news came into the English camp the day before, that the Turks had dynamited the city and proposed to touch it off as the English army entered; of course placing the blame on the English. The general called his staff together and said to them. "The only hope is in prayer to God." And next day when they marched into the city they found it vacated and that God had given them full deliverance without the fire of a gun. This should put a note of praise and thanksgiving into every Christian heart.

I have often been asked if it would increase or decrease a man's faith in God and the Bible to visit the Holy Land. My reply has been if a man is an intelligent Christian, knowing the Old and New Testament Scriptures, prophecies and their literal fulfillment, it would increase his faith in the divine authenticity of the Scriptures and the right that the Christian Church has to live and prosper throughout the world. On the other hand, if he does not know the Scriptures, when he looks upon the destitute condition, the illiteracy, the superstition and the filthiness of the country and people, it will increase his unbelief and cause the infidel to ridicule the Christian's God and the land where He has done His most marvelous works in the establishment of Christianity. The superstitions based on traditions, in that country are appalling, perplexing and distressing. The greatest atheist that I have known in my native state, visited that country the year after I did and came back and wrote a book on the country entitled "Dog Fennel in the Orient," which meant to me that all he got out of the Holy Land was as useless to the world as the pestiferous dog fennel in "Ole Kentuck." "The fool has said in his heart there is no God," and no amount of truth can convince such a one to the contrary.

After spending twelve days in the historic city we went back to Joppa, thence up the Sharon Valley to Keifer, a town on the northern side of Mount Carmel in the Esdraelon Valley. From Keifer we took a hack through the Esdraelon Valley, often mountains on either side, to the little town of Cana of Galilee where Jesus wrought His first miracle. There I saw a shepherd boy bring his sheep down, as his ancestors had done for centuries, to water and take them back to the mountains. From there we went to Nazareth, a town of ten thousand people, nestling at the base of the mountains. This was the most filthy town I saw in that country. We took dinner at this place, and from here went to the Sea of Galilee. On the east and west were mountains, from which when we were looking down into the Sea of Galilee it seemed as if we were but a few hundred yards away. I was tempted to jump out of the hack and run down the mountain, when the driver assured me we were three miles away from it. The Sea of Galilee is an enlargement of the river Jordan which has four sources about fifty miles away. The sea is about six miles in width and twelve miles in length. The old cities of Korazin upon a mountain northwest of the sea, Capernaum at the northwest side of the lake, and Bethsaida, a short distance on the west side of the sea, have only enough of the debris left to show great ruins, reminding the Bible student of the statement of Jesus: "Woe unto thee, Chorazin! woe unto thee Bethsaida! for if the mighty works had been done in Tyre and Sidon, which have been done in you, they had a great while ago repented, sitting in sackcloth and ashes. But it shall be more tolerable for Tyre and Sidon at the judgment, than for you. And thou, Capernaum, which art exalted to heaven, shalt be thrust down to hell."

We spent the night at Tiberius on the west side of the Sea of Galilee, and next day took a train on its first trip back to Keifer, and took our boat there for Port Said. We took off our hats as we saw the last of the Bible land, and hoped that if we should never see the Jerusalem of Palestine or the Holy Land again that we should see the New Jerusalem occupied by the Triune God, the angels and the redeemed of the Lord of all countries and in all ages that shall live in perfect harmony through the cycles of all eternity.

CHAPTER XV.

HOMEWARD BOUND.

We left the historic land of Palestine at the little town of Keifer where Mt. Carmel projects into the Mediterranean Sea, about fifteen hours' ride to Port Said, Egypt. Our next objective point was Naples, Italy, about four days' ride, passing close by Sicily and Stromboli a live volcano, which we had seen in our outgoing trip, which looks through a field glass like a large hay stack in a meadow. A little city at its base which appeared to be a white border, and the crater pouring out hot lava, seemed to be a peculiar place to build a town, but many similar cases occur in the Old Country. The Bible students will readily remember that this was the route taken by Paul on his trips to Rome. We are now again at Naples for a short stay.

A large portion of Pompeii has been exhumed, some of the specimens preserved, which brought vividly to our minds the just punishment of God on cities that had utterly ignored Him, treating themselves as beasts rather than human beings. Many of the walls were still standing with pictures drawn on them, showing their style of art. These things confirmed me in a long standing opinion, that much of ancient art, both sculpture and painting, savors more of paganism than of Christianity. Out of the 30,000 inhabitants of Pompeii, 27,000 were destroyed

HOMEWARD BOUND 159

by the terrible volcanic eruption, and buried beneath its burning lava. I saw a number of human bodies as natural in their petrified state as they were in their original state. I saw a dog that, when the fire struck him, was biting himself on the side, as natural as if he were still alive. Herculaneum has but little been exhumed. Through a channel opened up in this buried city we went to a theater. It was in a good state of preservation.

Leaving Naples, about a twelve hour run landed us in the eternal city on seven hills looking down on the Tiber. We first visited St. Peter's Cathedral. It was immense in proportions, without seats except in some small chapels. The main building was largely steadied with great rows of huge columns. I made several visits to this historical church when there was no service and when there was service. St. Peter's statue stood in a conspicuous place and his nose had been kissed off by the devotees of the church. The thoughtful tourists were first impressed with the sacredness of the Virgin Mary, then St. Peter, finally of Jesus whose image generally presented him either in the act of crucifixion or some other condition, impressing the tourists that they worshipped alone a dead Christ, not a victorious living Christ.

Adjoining the great Cathedral is the Vatican. I feel disposed to call it the Pope's den, as he claims to be a prisoner. It is a respectable building of eleven thousand rooms, where having no family he certainly has all the solitude his bachelor heart craves. I visited this one day spending several hours, but of course, visited only a small portion. It is no wonder to me that Luther was so disgusted when he made his first visit to Rome that he was driven to the Bible conclusion, "The just shall live by faith," and that he should go back to Wittenberg and publish his ninety-five theses repudiating jusification by works, and announcing what proved to be the germ of the Reformation, "Justification by faith." Of course, I visited the old Forum where Cicero used to hurl in thunder tones his matchless orations. Overshadowed on the one side by the Palatine hills and on the other by the Capitoline hills, where Cæsar lost his life by his enemies, and his pretended friend, Brutus. No wonder that when he saw Brutus as one of his slayers he said, "And thou too, Brutus?" His ambition was taken away and his faith in man destroyed, though it was an abnormal ambition. It is a calamity to any man to lose his normal ambition, and his faith in his fellowman. Close by the Forum were the ruins of the Colosseum, the most extraordinary ruins I had ever seen, a room that would contain ninety thousand people, an inhuman, diabolical resort to furnish entertainment to a godless world. I visited different parts of the city each morning while I was in Rome. Not far from the Colosseum was the cell in which Paul was imprisoned, made of limestone rock, and remains intact to this day. As our guide took us through it there was a large niche in the rock, and he informed us that that niche broken in the rock was done by a stroke of Paul's head, being knocked down by a soldier whom he had insulted. Such are the stories that abound in all those countries. The same guide on the Appian Way pointed us to the spot where he said Jesus and Peter had a noted conversation. When I informed him that no man's head was as hard as rock, and that Jesus, as a man, never was in Rome, very probably Peter was never there, his reply was that that was what he had been taught to say. While on the Appian Way we took in the Catacombs, long channels cut in stone quite a distance under the earth's surface, with niches cut on the sides to place the dead bodies. After spending several hours with the guide and my fellow tourists in these damp and dark quarters, with the bones of former inhabitants for thousands of years, one of the tourists said to me, "It is awfully lonesome in here, isn't it?" I replied, "It surely is. These men have not been very communicative for several thousand years."

We left Rome in about a week, making a hurried trip to Florence. We took in some of its most interesting points. Remembering most vividly the life and tortuous death of the first martyr of the Reformation, Savonarola, who died for the truth.

Our next city was Venice, on the Adriatic Sea, a town situated on islands, with watery streets constantly crowded with gondolas, therefore the quietest city in the world. You get in and out of your hotel from a gondola and do not hear the sound of a horse or a vehicle. Of course, it is a city of cathedrals, and churches and art galleries. The most noted place we visited was the House of Dodges, that is, the rulers of the city, and headquarters of that diabolical inquisition instigated during the dark ages by the Roman Catholic Church. Adjoining this building were the places of torture and Bridge of Sighs, across which, its prisoners passed to the place of execution, seeing light for the last time. I was asked in the presence of a guide, "Who did this persecuting?" I replied, "The Roman Catholic Church, of course." It so offended him that he asked me to pay him off and he would go, and this I promptly did.

From Venice we went to Milan. We saw but little of this city. As my custom was, I arose at five o'clock and put in two hours touring before breakfast. Not planning to stay in the city but a few hours, I took a walk from my hotel, and failed to retain the name and location, took a hack and visited the most noted cathedral in the world, said to be the largest and most magnificent Gothic structure in the world. Three hundred and fifty-five feet high, built of marble, its entire length six hundred and eighty-four feet, it has ninety-two spires and three thousand pieces of statuary on the exterior. I got lost that morning. My cabman could not understand English, and as I failed to get the name and location of the hotel, all I could say was, "Take me back to where you found me." This I repeated several times with a loud voice and strong gesticulation, hoping by so doing to beat it into him. In despair I made him stop his hack; ran into a hotel and said. "Is there a man here who understands English?" A gentleman replied in English. I said "Of all men in the world I want to see, you are the man, for I am lost, and I cannot make this man understand where he found me." I said, "Tell him to take me back where he found me." They had a big laugh at my expense, and motioned me to get in, and in fifteen minutes I was at my hotel door.

We boarded an early train for Switzerland that took us, in common with the previous day, through more tunnels than any day's travel in my life. A good portion of the day we were in sight of the Alps; beautiful, but not so rugged as our Rockies. I complained to the railroad captain about the numerous tunnels. He said, "You will have more today than you did yesterday, ending your day going through a tunnel nine miles in length." Entering Switzerland in a beautiful mountain town, located on Lake Lucerne, we found it one of the prettiest, with picturesque environments, everlastingly crowned with snow.

From Lucerne we started for France, taking in a little corner of Germany, thence through that beautiful agricultural country of France, to its noted capital, which is beautiful for situation, streets, boulevards, great architectural skill, crowded with historic art galleries, museums, churches and cathedrals. As a relic of the Revolution, we were pointed to a place known as "hell" and another as "heaven," and still another known as "nowhere." Of course, it was a caricature of the Bible and Christianity; the rejection of which was the cause of the bloody revolution, and brought to our minds their infidel burlesque, both on God and the Bible, by tying the Bible to the tail of an ass, and running it up and down the streets of Paris. The footprints of the devil and his work have been stamped upon that country in a good measure ever since, notwithstanding their learning and great intellectual enlightenment. We spent several days visiting many of the most noted places in the city. Crossing the English Channel, the English people and country reminded us more of the United States than any other country we had seen.

Reaching London, then the largest city in the world, (now New York surpasses it), we spent a week in viewing the points that were of most interest to us; art galleries, museums, great banks, cathedrals, giving special attention to St. Paul's Cathedral, the highest observatory in the city. I climbed seven hundred steps to where I had the finest possible view of the city. As I went down I took in the whispering gallery, where a man stood at one side of the wall and said, "Sir Christopher Wren was the architect of St. Paul's Cathedral." (What a versatile life he had followed!) The tourists standing one hundred feet away by the other wall could hear the sound as if it came out of the wall near them. I then visited Westminster Abbey, one of the most noted Protestant Cathedrals of the world, the resting place of England's most noted dead, many of them placed underneath the floor, and statues by the thousand, including the busts of John and Charles Wesley, which made me feel at least that they had a little respect for old-fashioned Christianity. The building inside and out is beautiful. Their invisible choir makes the most beautiful music I ever heard from the human voice, particularly to our aesthetic nature. I visited Charles H. Spurgeon's church, occupied by his son, Thomas Spurgeon; heard Thomas Spurgeon preach to four thousand people, led by a choir of a hundred and fifty, not a musical instrument in the house, the entire congregation supplied with hymn books. This singing was unequaled by any I heard on the line of real worship on that side of the Atlantic. The pastor preached a good spiritual sermon. Many "amens" were heard during the discourse. I was informed by one of the elders who introduced me to the pastor that they had had soul-saving work going on every week since the establishment of that church. I could but thank God for Charles H. Spurgeon, that Spirit-filled Baptist who was big enough for all religious denominations to claim an interest in him.

By means of a permit that I received from Mr. Roosevelt, then President, through a Congressional friend of mine, I visited the Parliament, both houses, drawing a comparison between them and our United States Capitol and Congress. I also had the privilege of visiting City Road Chapel, standing in Mr. Wesley's pulpit, visiting his tomb, which was near that of Adam Clarke, Joseph Benson, and some other notable men. I also visited the little room of five by six feet, known as Wesley's prayer room, where he prayed down the great Methodist revival. Adjoining this room was the room where he did his writing and planning when at home, and from which he went to Heaven.

I separated from my fellow tourists and took in Glasgow and Edinburgh, visiting a few noted places in these cities, especially the John Knox home where he uttered that noted sentence, "Give me Scotland or I die." I also visited some places where Thomas Carlyle's footprints still remain. The Scotch people were a serious, thoughtful, moral, courteous people as I saw them in my flying trip. I also took a flying trip to the Emerald Isle, visiting Dublin and Belfast, the latter a noted ship building city. I took in a great deal of the country which exhibited the poorest prospect for agriculture of any country I visited.

I took ship at Queenstown, meeting my fellow tourists who had taken ship at Liverpool for our dear old United States. So soon as I entered the ship I was introduced by one of my fellow tourists to an old gentleman from Pennsylvania who was to be an occupant of the same room as ourselves. Finding out what State we were from, out of the kindness of his heart I presume, he occupying a lower berth, pulled out of his suitcase from under it a long black bottle, which he assured us was the best in the market, taking out the stopper, saying,

"I never saw a Kentuckian that didn't like the looks of this." As I was the oldest of our company, I replied, "Well, you are completely mistaken this time, for we are Kentucky tee-totalers and Methodist ministers, and anti-tobacconists, and neither drink nor smoke." When he saw I was in earnest about it he put the stopper in the bottle and the bottle in his suitcase, and said, "I'm in it, ain't I?" I said, "You surely are for the next three thousand miles." We reached the United States and were soon back in old Kentucky again.

CHAPTER XVI.

KINGSWOOD COLLEGE.

COLLEGE MOTTO: (Common sense, Industry, Bible Salvation insure success for Time and Eternity.)

After a half year of honest thinking and praying, in a state of constant indecision, as to my future work, I heard of a large farm in Southwestern Kentucky that would possibly make a good location for a school; that section of the country was in need of a school, and too, it was away from the whirl of confusion and sin of city life, and where students could have constant fellowship and communion with nature as well as with college professors and books. I immediately felt drawn to investigate the farm, and felt that God was in the message that called my attention to it for the location of a college. It was sixty-five miles from Louisville, Kentucky; three miles from a branch road of the L. H. and St. L. Railroad. I bought the farm of about one thousand acres on which to build my second full salvation school and camp meeting.

I arrived at this place with my family and household goods on January 17, 1906. I found a two-story log house, weather-boarded, built in the antebellum days, which had been the home of slave holders. The negro cabins originally on the hills above. I also found three large barns; a horse and mule barn; a cattle barn; and a large tobacco barn with all their fixtures.

There were a number of tenant houses occupied by those who cultivated the farm. The first thing I did after getting adjusted in our new quarters was to dispose of the tobacco tenants. For under no circumstances could I have tobacco cultivated on the farm. I used these tenants in converting a large part of the woodland on the place into lumber; the stone of the cliffs into building foundations, and putting in a saw mill and planing mill on the farm; using all kinds of mechanics that had to do with housebuilding. I employed from thirty to forty hands for about eight months in constructing our college buildings. I told my workers at the beginning that I would do all the fussing, "cussing," and lounging that was to be done, that I expected to treat every man as a gentleman and friend, and pay them good wages and expected them to make good at whatever job they were assigned. I have seen on the farm at work at one time, twenty head of horses, mules and oxen, used in cultivating the land, hauling saw logs, lumber, stone, sand and all kinds of building material.

My two lieutenants were Rev. P. C. Long and Rev. F. T. Howard, young men that were studying for the ministry. They were young men of good judgment, indomitable energy, Spirit-filled, absolutely reliable, out of as well as in your sight. No man perhaps ever had truer men to assist in a great undertaking. These two young men are now members of the Kentucky Conference, and among our most reliable pastors and soul winners. They made the impression then among that collection of mechanics, that they were God's men and that impression continues in their pastoral and revival work. I love them almost as my own boys. Though it was reported that my health had broken down in Asbury College, it was never better, as I prosecuted the work with these two young men. We got the major part of these buildings completed by the 20th of August. I kept a horse saddled and reviewed the entire work two or three times a day, seeing that everything was kept in order.

In the meantime we had built a brush arbor in which to start our camp meeting. The twentieth day of August the camp meeting was begun, resulting in about 150 conversions and sanctifications. We had an old-fashioned, God-endorsed, full salvation camp meeting for the ten years that I remained in charge of the work.

Our college campus was one of the most beautiful I ever saw. My now sainted friend, Dr. C. J. Fowler, of Boston, said he had not seen it surpassed any where, and I think that was the judgment of all who saw it. All our buildings were wooden structures. The college buildings and president's residence were heated with hot air; the boys' and girls' dormitories with stoves. They were plain, but respectable and comfortable. The work at Kingswood was begun the same as Asbury College, as my own private property.

Our first year's enrollment was one hundred and seven. The entire year's work was marked with a

KINGSWOOD COLLEGE 171

good degree of success, making a fine impression upon my constituency in the county and adjoining counties. Quite a number of students came from different states.

After much thought and prayer we named the institution Kingswood College, for Kingswood School established by John Wesley and George Whitefield among the miners of England, that being the first school established in the Great Methodist Movement. Many of my friends have said to me that while its location is a little inconvenient, the name and objective were splendidly selected and deserving of success. Like Asbury College, it was on trial by the church and outsiders for a number of years as it continued its normal growth. One man said no school could ever succeed so far from a railroad and town. I reminded him of what was said of Mark Hopkins, "That Mark Hopkins on one end of a log and a boy on the other end constituted a university."

The men and women associated with me in the faculty did a class of work on all educational lines that thoroughly commended itself to the public, educators, ministers of the Gospel, and, especially such talent as I brought to assist me in camp meeting, college revivals and commencements. And also the class of young men and women that constituted the student body, and its graduates that have gone out as teachers, preachers and missionaries, to say nothing of young gentlemen and ladies in other vocations in life.

The people backed by the student body, my ministerial, and teacher friends and teaching force, soon put the school beyond the experimental state, and it was generally conceded that it had a perfect right not only to live, but to have the encouragement and patronage of all religious and right thinking people. I do not hesitate to say that we turned out from Kingswood College some of the most promising and useful young men and women that I have ever known, having creditable records as scholars, ministers, teachers, and other professions in life. They have made splendid records in some of the leading universities in this country. One young man went to one of the leading universities in this country after graduating from Kingswood College, to take a medical course, and took with honors his five year course in four years. In the meantime he had presented his diploma that he had received from Kingswood to the Dean of the Scientific Department, asking him on what terms he could get his Bachelor of Science degree. The Dean replied, "On the ground that you take the entire course, as the diplomas you have do not count in this university, for there are but a few schools in Kentucky whose diplomas are taken for their face value." He took the scientific course while working on his medical degree, and when the Dean of that department gave him his degree he said, "Your work is of so high a grade that you fully deserve the degree, and tell the President of that institution that whenever a student comes to us in the future with a diploma signed by him, that that student will be received with the face value of the diploma." Certainly demonstrating the fact that first-class work was being done at Kingswood College. Another young man came to us from a barber's chair in the South. He took one of our degrees and later going to one of our universities, entered the Theological department with the purpose of taking his B. D. degree. On his entrance examination he was required to read and translate fifty lines of Greek that he had never seen before, which he did by looking up two or three words, and they put him to teaching Greek the next day. He stood at the head of his work throughout his theological course, taking while there his Master of Arts degree, as well as his B. D. He was then requested to become a teacher in the institution and now has the chair of education in one of our large southern colleges.

Many of the students as teachers, preachers, missionaries, and other responsible positions in life have high places of trust in home and in foreign lands. Many pastors are serving good charges in the conference in different parts of this country, and contending for the faith once delivered to the saints.

Many who did not graduate have been soul winners, going through the country as flames of fire, getting hundreds, and all told, thousands of people to God. Notably one man thirty-five years of age came to us with a wife and three children. He could neither read nor write. He asked me if I could make anything out of such a man. My reply to him was, "If you have three things, we can." He said, "What are the three things?" I said, "Industry, common sense, and salvation." He said to me, "Explain to me what you mean." I said, "Industry means that you are not lazy." His reply was, "I can meet that." "The next is Bible salvation." He replied. "I am saved, sanctified, and called to preach, glory to God." I said, "The last is common sense, which means, as a farmer, if you were feeding the pigs you'd put the food into the trough rather than on your breeches." His reply was, "I know I have that much sense." He has already been the instrument in the hands of God in winning hundreds to God, being one of the most useful evangelists in the territory where he works, that I know of.

Our enrollment for a number of years ran from a hundred and fifty to one hundred and seventy-nine. Most of the time fifty or more were studying for the ministry.

One of the wealthiest men in Breckenridge County, in which Kingswood College is located, said to me, "The greatest thing that ever struck Breckenridge County is your Kingswood College project." Referring to the combined work of the school, camp meeting, and evangelistic work in that and adjoining counties, in a radius of thirty miles there were at least three thousand people saved or sanctified, and hundreds added to the church. The nine years (ten counting the year of its construction) that I was connected with the school we had a constant revivalistic spirit in the school. The last time I heard from the school it had two hundred students and was doing good work.

For several years I was aware that the financial and mental pressure along with my teaching and general superintendence of the school, with the constant solicitude for the salvation and the preparation of the student body for the work of God, would finally break down my nerves. I finally prayed through to God and received the assurance from Him that my work as a college president was soon coming to an end. Notwithstanding the persistent effort of the people to get me to remain as the president of the school, I felt that I owed it to myself, and to any possible usefulness that I might have in the future, to retire from the burdensome work— the work I loved as no other work in the world—that of getting young life in touch with God and prepared for the Master's work.

I was offered, after I left Kingswood College, the presidency of three good full salvation schools, and chairs of theology and philosophy were offered me a number of times, but I felt that I dare not confine myself to constant schedule work. I think I could have done some light work, possibly more efficiently than I ever did, being relieved from all financial pressure and burdens, incident to the headship of a school. Nevertheless, I felt possibly that whatever usefulness I had in me I would do most for the world in devoting my time and strength largely to writing, leaving some of the results of my student and teacher life in permanent form in books to be read while living and after I shall have gone. I am now hoping with some pulpit and platform work, and with what work I can do through the press, I may conclude my life's work. First, in creating a Memorial Loan Fund for young ministers and prospective missionaries in Asbury College that will continue in some little measure my educational work in years to come. I also hope soon to have out my life story in connection with the histories of Asbury and Kingswood Colleges. My prayer to God is that each book as it is sent to different parts of the world, particularly to my old students, their parents and other full salvation people that are interested in the promotion of holiness may read and get others to read the book, that it may lead hundreds of young men and women to know God, and fully consecrate themselves to the work under the call of God to save as far as possible all men from all sin.

I close this sketch with the following story, which is one of the sweetest memories in my ministerial and school life. A gentleman about my age was one of my tenants for a number of years. He had never discovered himself, nor had been discovered by anyone; a man of remarkable ability, a born wit and humorist, a natural gentleman, but with little educational cultivation. He got gloriously saved and sanctified. This in a measure (though late in life) discovered him to himself and to others. He felt called to preach at once. He was a

BIRD'S EYE VIEW OF KINGSWOOD CAMPUS.

thoughtful, successful preacher from the beginning, having extraordinary evangelistic gifts, a real soul winner. In a few years he won hundreds of souls to God, often walking sixteen miles to his appointment. He used to say to me, "If your coming to Kingswood did nothing else but get me saved it would pay you for coming." He came to me one day apparently in good health, and said, "I am having a little financial struggle now. I came to see if you would let me cut some railroad ties on your place," saying that he would cut and haul them to the depot and divide equally with me. I replied that I did not want those trees cut. He said with a trembling voice and with tears in his eyes, "I don't know then what I am to do to take care of my family." I loved him as a brother, and could not stand his tears and the tremor of his voice. I then said, "Go and cut anything you please. Get all you can out of it. Take care of yourself and family." When we separated we were both in tears. Little did I then know how close he was to eternity, for the next morning at six o'clock he slipped away victoriously to Heaven. I saw that he was nicely prepared with a burial outfit, preached his funeral to a large congregation of sympathizing, loving friends, all of whom said, "Uncle Alec went all right." I expect to meet him in Heaven in the not distant future with hundreds he had led to God.

CHAPTER XVII.

AS A THEOLOGICAL TEACHER.

From time immemorial the scholasticus, school master or teacher has been a familar figure in the forward march of the world's civilization. He trains, educates, directs the unlearned and unlettered into the pathway of understanding, imparts knowledge and gives instruction. He chases away the nightmare of ignorance before the rosy dawn of progress and bears the torch of intelligence to the ends of the earth. The great men of history, recognizing the value and validity of knowledge, have always congratulated and complimented the efficient teacher. Napoleon said that the first duty of every republic is the education of its youth. Edmond Burke looked on education as a chief defense of nations. Cicero, the Roman orator, in one of his perfervid and forensic speeches highly honored and ably defended his old teacher the poet Archaeus. Aristotle, the famous father of logic, was the honored teacher of Alexander the Great. Alcuin, the Christian scholar, was the teacher of Charlemagne, that most conspicious, outstanding, secular and imperial character of the middle ages. Rabbanus, the foremost pupil of Alcuin, was honored and spoken of as the first preceptor of Germany.

Without doing violence to the facts of history we may classify the Greek philosophers, in all their

AS A THEOLOGICAL TEACHER 179

grand array, as so many teachers. They taught their respective systems of philosophy.

We owe a debt of gratitude to the true teacher under whatever name he may be known—principal, pedagogue, professor, tutor, educator, instructor.

Thomas Jefferson, the sage of Monticello and the penman of the immortal Declaration of Independence said, "If a nation expects to be ignorant and free in a state of civilization it expects what never was and never will be."

Daniel Webster, the matchless orator and American statesman of literary learning, made the following statement, "On the diffusion of education among the people rests the preservation and perpetuation of free institutions."

John Jay said, "I consider knowledge to be the soul of the Republic."

Horace Mann declared that the common school was the greatest discovery made by man.

But in all the far-flung line of educational training, whether scientific, classical or philosophical, theology is evidently the greatest of all. Nature is the field of physical sciences; man is the subject of mental and moral philosophy, while God is the lofty theme of theology.

With these preliminary statements on education in general we come now to consider the caliber, qualification and career of J. W. Hughes as a theological teacher. His first experience in the art of instruction dates back to the time when he was an Owen County school teacher. In life's changing vicissitudes he went from the teacher's desk to the pastor's pulpit and from the pastor's pulpit to the evangelist's platform, and from the evangelist's platform into the theological professor's chair. The following query, relative to Doctor Hughes' technical teaching ability, may be propounded by some people, "Was Doctor Hughes a real teacher in the true sense of the term, or was he just a good exhorter and preacher before his pupils?" The answer to this question depends a great deal upon the different definitions and conceptions of a *bona fide* theological professor. What does it take to constitute a genuine, four-square, full-fledged professor in Biblical science? If one has to divide up the historical periods of theological thought into the rabbinic, hellenistic, patristic, individualistic, dogmatic and modern and take his stand in the modern era, the unmistakable earmarks of which are rationalism, criticism, liberalism and Darwinism, and cut the virus out of sin, the fire out of hell, the blood out of the atonement, the miraculous out of the Old Testament, the authority out of the New, the prediction out of prophecy, the infallibility out of inspiration and the supernatural out of religion in order to be dubbed as a first class professor in the theological world, then Doctor Hughes could not measure up to the so-called modern standard of Theological professorship.

If one has to be a regular Dutch-cheese, Limburger, Wellhausen, higher critic and biological baboon booster in order to be recognized as an

AS A THEOLOGICAL TEACHER 181

able and efficient teacher in the Theological Seminaries of the different denominations of Christendom, then Doctor Hughes again falls short of official professorship.

If one has to speak in sepulchral tones and put on professional airs, walk in a stately or stilted manner, wisely roll his eyes in owl-like solemnity and look dignified, daring and dogmatically dangerous in order to be a formal professor of the first waters, then Doctor Hughes will never quite qualify. If one has to be nice and precise, dilettante and dude-like, with his hair parted in the middle and his whiskers sharpened down to such a fine point that he could thread a cambric needle, deal in glittering generalities and empty platitudes and be diplomatic, indefinite and undogmatic in dealing with the great cardinal doctrines of the Bible in order to be a real true teacher of theology, then Doctor Hughes would stand no chance of professional promotion.

If one must have a profound knowledge of Hebrew and Sanskrit, the unmitigated gall and personal pluck to pick the Bible to pieces, the moral courage to criticize the divinely-inspired apostles and prophets, entertaining the Pyrronian doubt and possess the so-called modern scientific spirit in order to be a past-master in theology, a preferred professor, then Doctor J. W. Hughes, we are proud to say, is not, never was, and never will be a professor of that sort. While Dr. Hughes did not meet the above requirements, all of which one may possess and yet not be a real true professor in the proper sense of the term, he had all the essential qualities and necessary qualifications that go to constitute a competent efficient professor of systematic theology. He was always clear and definite on every proposition; he was positive and pronounced on the great fundamental principles of theological thought; he was both instructive and constructive, but never destructive. We do not hesitate in affirming that he was one of the very foremost theological teachers of his day. He knew what he wanted; he knew where to find it; and he knew what to do with it after he had received it. The following outline will help us to size up the man, to sum up his points, and to mark his distinguishing traits as a technical teacher in the field of theological thought.

1. He was richly endowed with natural teaching ability. It is said that poets must be born, not made. The same thing is true in regard to other professions. We speak of born orators, born leaders, and born preachers. Why not include teachers in the list? A real genuine, true teacher must have a native gift in order to be an adept and expert in the art of instruction. His natural endowment must be such as to enable him to tell what he knows in a plain, positive, forceful, expressive and emphatic manner. Dr. Hughes was favored in this regard.

2. He was not only endowed by nature with innate powers and teaching tendencies, but was educationally qualified and equipped as a theological professor. In addition to the regular Conference Course

AS A THEOLOGICAL TEACHER 183

in connection with his ministry he attended the Kentucky Wesleyan College, had three and one-half years in Greek, and graduated from Vanderbilt University in Moral Philosophy. His diploma from that institution in the year 1880 reads: "To whom it may concern, greeting: Be it known that J. W. Hughes has attained the required standard in the full course of study in the School of Moral Philosophy in this University, in testimony whereof, this certificate of proficiency has been this day conferred upon him under the seal and authority of the University." Signed by J. C. Garland, Chancellor; J. C. Granberry, teacher, afterward Bishop. This document, or diploma, speaks for itself. It serves to correct any false idea afloat to the effect that Dr. Hughes was not fully trained and scientifically educated. The fact is, he had a first class education in his special field of instruction. He never posed as a teacher on any line except theology and metaphysics. He selected and secured a fine faculty to teach the arts and sciences, while he himself occupied the chair of theology and moral philosophy.

3. A theological professor, in order to be efficient in the full sense of the word must have more than mere book learning. He must first know God for himself in a personal religious experience before he can properly and impressively teach the deeper spiritual truths to others. A dry, formal intellectualist may teach tenets, dogmas, and theories, but he cannot correctly and consistently impart the deeper things of theology. The theological

teacher, in the true sense of the term, is one of the Divinely constituted orders of the Christian ministry. "He gave some apostles, some prophets, some evangelists, some pastors and teachers." (Eph. 4:11-13.) A true teacher must first sit at the feet of the Master and know his Lord from an experimental standpoint in order to be a full-fledged competent teacher of systematic theology. The education of the head without the heart invariably leads to formalism and rationalism. This is the trouble with the modern higher critical professors of the present day. On the other hand the education of the heart without the head leads to wild fire and fanaticism. Dr. Hughes happily struck the Golden Mean and persistently maintained the view that every man should be educated not only in mind and muscle, but in heart and soul. His sky-blue conversion, and subsequent sanctification contributed much toward the completion of a full-orbed theological professor. In order to be an ideal doctrinaire in the best sense of the word one must teach with the Holy Ghost sent down from Heaven.

4. Being definitely called to collegiate work, he was providentially inspired to take up the great task of teaching and training young men for the ministry. While he was remarkably successful in the pastorate and most efficient in the evangelistic field, he felt that hundreds could do more than one. Hence, he concluded to give the best and most of his time in training and sending out ministers and missionaries to the ends of the world. So the Provi-

dence of God was with him as he stood before his students to teach them the great fundamental and cardinal doctrines of Christianity.

5. He had unbounded energy and overwhelming enthusiasm. All the faculties of mind, soul, and body were brought into requisition and laid under contribution when he tackled the task of teaching theology and metaphysics. He did not lazily sit back in the professor's easy chair and quietly and calmly ask a few questions on the lesson, and leave the pupils to draw their own conclusions. But like the Master, he taught as one having authority, and not as the scribes and Pharisees. He did not deal in pale perhapses, probabilities, and uncertainties, but with vim and vigor he put forth verities and positive principles. He powerfully impressed his pupils that he believed and practiced what he taught.

6. Another thing that helped and enhanced his teaching was the readiness and eagerness on the part of his pupils to learn. It is said that beauty lies in the landscape and waits for the painter's eye, that the block of marble smiles as the sculptor passes by. Dr. Hughes, having founded the first Holiness College in the land, gathered around him a group of young men and women who, for the most part, were sober, serious, and tremendously in earnest on the subject of education. They were eager to learn in order that they might get out into the work and make good in their respective callings. The same Divine Power which assisted Dr. Hughes

in teaching these pupils also assisted them in learning theology. As it is easier to preach to a prayed-up campmeeting crowd than to a cold, dead, formal, indifferent church audience, so it is easier to teach this kind of a student body than the average college student body of the day.

7. The kind of a text book one teaches has much to do with his success as a teacher. We cannot expect much from many of the modern text books. They are saturated with rationalism and Darwinism. It is hard for a stream to rise above its source. Dr. Hughes acted wisely in the selection of great standard text books for his theological students. The curriculum included Ralston's Elements of Divinity, Butler's Analogy, and Hamiltons Metaphysics. There is no better book than Ralston for teaching the elements of Divinity or the fundamentals of Christian Theology. It contains more real sound Gospel Theology than a dozen of the modern text books, even though a professor of Vanderbilt University recently ridiculed it with the insinuation that it might do as much good as "Ralston's" breakfast food. But Dr. R. A. Meek, Editor of the Southern Methodist, quite the reverse of the Vanderbilt professor, says: "In this day when there is much confusion in our religious teaching, we think it would be well for our young ministers to procure and carefully read Dr. Ralston's great work. It is worth a whole shelf of the common run of theological treatises being issued from our presses in this day." Butler's Analogy was one of the great

outstanding productions of the eighteenth century, a great classic, a clarion call to complete confidence in revealed as well as natural religion, a masterful defense of the Faith of our Fathers. It practically dealt a death-blow to English Deism and turned back the tide of infidelity for a solid century. Dr. Hughes delighted to carry his pupils into the deep truths of the "Analogy." Hamilton's Metaphysics is a product of stupendous erudition. It deals with the great problems of philosophy. It takes more than an ordinary man to intelligently teach and interestingly instruct pupils in the ponderous truths of Hamilton's Metaphysics. But Dr. Hughes was equal to the task.

8. If a theological teacher has dialectical skill it only adds to his general qualifications as a religious instructor. He is therefore not only able to teach the tenets of a certain system of doctrine, but is ready to defend them against all comers in the open forum of religious controversy. Dr. Hughes was rooted and grounded in the great fundamental doctrines of Methodism, and was ready to meet any opponent in a pitched battle on the planes of polemical discussion. On this line Dr. A. Redd says of him: "As a defender of the faith he wields a keen blade. We acted moderator for him in a debate which he held at Wilmore with Elder Howe, of the Christian Church. The Elder was a champion of his denomination—had held several debates—had experience. His specialty was repartee. But in this he was no match for Dr. Hughes. His sallies

sounded chestnutty beside Dr. Hughes' retorts, which born of the moment, gleamed like stilettos. It was evident that the Elder came off second best." Elder J. W. Howe was a former lawyer and a fierce antagonist. He had debated with the president of Georgetown College. He had held twenty-five debates, it is claimed, before he met Dr. Hughes. The Wilmore debate lasted four days. During the discussion the Elder told the audience that he was going to trot out in his next speech a little "black pony"—the Methodist Discipline. To which Dr. Hughes replied: "Very well, trot him out if you dare, for I, too, am going to trot out an "old plug"—the Campbellite Discipline." Whereupon the respective "war horses"—the two creeds—were marched out into the arena. The Elder did not fancy the "plug" and tried to deny his pedigree, but Dr Hughes made him come across, and convinced the congregation that the Campbellites had a creed in the form of the "Christian Discipline"—written by Alexander Campbell in 1835.

The Elder in one of his speeches, compared Dr. Hughes with his tenacity to the bull-pups he used to raise at his father's home. Dr. Hughes' retort took the Elder off his feet. "I think, ladies and gentlemen, that Elder Howe missed his calling. He should have continued raising bull-pups on his father's farm instead of trying to preach the Gospel." The Elder rallied and declared that if some one would pin Dr Hughes' ears back and grease him that he would swallow him whole. Then Dr. Hughes forever demolished the daring and dashing elder with the discomfiting reply: "If he should swallow me, there is one thing certain, he would have more brains in his stomach than he has in his head." The debate was a great stimulus to the college and was a star in the controversial crown of its founder.

9. Dr. Hughes was not only a teacher and a controversialist, but a conversationalist on theological themes. One one occasion he engaged Dr. James M. Mudge, of Malden Massachusetts, in religious conversation. Dr. Mudge is a noted author and one of the brightest men of New England Methodism. Dr. Hughes led the conversation, which turned on the doctrine of full salvation. He presented the different phases of the subject in such a forceful and feasible way that the brilliant New England scholar practically agreed with him on all the essential points of the theory. In some respects it was similar to the noted conversation between John Wesley and the eminent Bishop of Durham. When John Wesley explained what he meant by entire sanctification—perfect love to God, and impartial love to man, the Bishop replied: "If that is all you mean, and if that is what you mean, then proclaim it to the whole world." On another occasion he engaged one of the biggest and brainiest bishops of the Methodist Episcopal Church, South, in conversation on the great cardinal doctrines of the Bible. In the course of the conversation Dr. Hughes proposed to the bishop to give a brief statement of what he taught his pupils at Asbury College. This opened the way

for Dr. Hughes to take the lead. He gained the bishop's assent, concurrence and congratulation on almost every point of his doctrinal dissertation. Other instances of his high intellectual conversational qualities might be cited, but these are sufficient to show that he was perfectly at home in the presence of profound theological thinkers.

10. The final test of a teacher's ability and skill is measured by the kind of goods he puts on the educational market in the form of the pupils he trains and turns out. Let us apply this practical test to J. W. Hughes. Did the students who went out from Asbury College during his presidential administration of the institution make their mark and amount to anything in the world? Ah, yes indeed! We can proudly point to a grand galaxy of early Asburians who have wrought well, achieved success, distinguished themselves, and reflected great honor upon the Institution. Fortunately, the very first graduate of the college laid the pattern and set the pace. He was easily the peer of any platform orator in the United States along the line of morality, perfect manhood, social purity, and eugenics. He is the author of a number of standard books on the subject of eugenics which have had an enormous sale, even the million mark has been passed. There is no college or university but what would be glad to have the honor of claiming the late Professor T. W. Shannon as one of its graduates. Next in order we mention Rev. W. C. Cram, D. D., Director General of the Centenary

AS A THEOLOGICAL TEACHER 191

Movement of the Methodist Episcopal Church, South. He has made a great record as one of the foremost missionaries in Korea. He stands today in the front rank of American Methodism.

Still high advanced stands that illustrious student, Stanley Jones; regarded by many as the most conspicuous and outstanding missionary in all India and the Far East. He has made an unparalleled record in reaching the high intellectual Hindu castes of India. He shines as a star of the first magnitude in the missionary world.

One of the most highly honored, hard-working, popular and effective missionary bishops of the great Methodist Episcopal Church, Fred B. Fisher, is another noted and illustrious graduate of Asbury under the Hughes' administration.

Prof. E. T. Franklin, Ph. D. A. M., president of Union College, Barboursville, Ky., is one of the most highly educated intellectual sons of Asbury. He is an alumnus of the class of 1903. He was one of Dr. Hughes' favorite students in the fair and fertile fields of metaphysical research.

Rev. L. R. Akers, D. D., former president of the Alumni Association, scholar, lecturer, pastor, teacher in the Methodist Summer Schools of Theology for the undergraduates, is another prominent graduate of Asbury College under the successful administration of Dr. Hughes.

Rev. Waskom Pickett is an honored graduate of Asbury under the old constitution. Waskom has made a great record as a missionary in India. He is a close second to Stanley Jones. He is the head of the prohibition movement for all India.

Rev. Luther B. Bridgers, D. D., traveler, lecturer and illustrious evangelist, was trained and educated under the guiding genius and instructive tutorage of Dr. J. W. Hughes. Luther Bridgers is a team within himself. He toured Europe, took in the lay of the land, sized up the situation, and came back with more first-hand, ready information than any man in the bounds of Southern Methodism. He also has the honor of having been the first General Evangelist of the M. E. Church, South.

Matsumoto, the famous Japanese student, who stands high in the official ranks of the Empire of the "Rising Sun," said to be third from the Mikado, sat at the feet of Dr. Hughes as one of his foreign boys.

Rev. Chas. H. Neal, a natural born organizer, an inventive genius, a gifted writer, a preacher of no mean ability, an honored pastor of the North Carolina Conference for a number of years, is another noted Asburian of the early order.

Rev. E. K. Pike, the well-known pastor-evangelist of the Kentucky Conference, a man of sterling worth and great stamina, true, tried and faithful, a powerful preacher and successful soul-winner, is a graduate of Asbury dating back in the good old days in the presidency of Dr. Hughes.

Rev. Will H. Huff, a prince of holiness evangelists, one of the greatest pulpiteers on the American Continent, got his start in Asbury College.

AS A THEOLOGICAL TEACHER 193

Rev. S. E. Edwards, a strong Gospel evangelist and successful missionary to Cuba and Central America, came out of Asbury under the efficient leadership of its founder and first president.

Rev. E. O. Chalfant, one of the prominent and gifted District Superintendents of the Nazarene Church, was a student under Dr. Hughes at Kingswood College.

Rev. H. W. Bromley, a brilliant man, a great revivalist, a keen writer, a learned lecturer, a prominent fundamentalist, is one of the early Asbury boys, an outstanding, polished pupil of Dr. Hughes.

Prof. M. L. Smith, a bright star in the intellectual realm, is a graduate of Kingswood College. He made one of the greatest records as a student in the history of Emory University. He now has the educational chair in the Methodist Female College, Montgomery, Ala.

Rev. W. L. Clark, D. D., a master builder, an organizing genius, an indefatigable worker, popular pastor, great preacher, business manager of Asbury College, is an honored graduate of the institution, trained and sent out by Dr. Hughes.

Rev. W. S. Maxwell, a man of strength, power, probity and principle, a strong preacher, a prominent pastor in the Kentucky Conference, is another honored Asbury boy who was theologically brought up at the feet of the father and founder of the institution.

Miss Pearl Mulligan, a deeply consecrated, Spirit-filled, consistent Christian, and a soul-winning missionary, Rhodesia, Africa, is an Asbury graduate, under Dr. Hughes, who reflects credit upon the institution.

Rev. F. B. Jones, the second graduate of the institution, has made a fine record in the home-land. He is a good preacher, a fine administrator, a level-headed, middle-of-the-road minister, a man who has lived his religion, and honored the institution. He is a Presiding Elder in the Kentucky Conference.

Rev. W. W. Shepherd, another Asbury boy, has made his mark in the world. He is a District Superintendent in the Kentucky Conference of the M. E. Church.

What shall I say more? Time would fail me to mention the full list.

It was a benediction to visit and to view Dr. Hughes at close range in his class room, to see him in didactive action. There sat the pupils ready for the recitation. Here comes the teacher, tuned up, toned up, and we might say, prayed up for the task. In the first place he calls on one of the members of the class to offer a short prayer. He then proceeds with the lesson. There is not a dull moment from start to finish. Questions are asked and answered. But this is the least of the program. The subject is analyzed, sifted, and searched. The minds of the pupils are focussed on the main points of the lesson. Various views and theories are discussed. Special truths and tenets are clarified and clinched with tremendous emphasis. The teacher explains, expounds, expostulates, dogmatizes, and indoctrinates. As a result of such plain, positive, and wholesome instruction the pupils go forth from the class room settled and established in the great fundamental truths of Christianity. How different from many modern professors who lead their students into metaphysical mazes and leave them in philosophical uncertainties! Dr. Hughes followed teaching, not as a profession, but as a calling. Like the Master, he taught as one having authority, and not as the scribes and Pharisees. In view of the foregoing facts he will forever go down in the history of the institution as its first, foremost, and highly favored theological professor.

At the recent Commencement of Asbury College Dr. Hughes was newly honored by the institution which he founded. The degree of Doctor of Divinity, a degree which he already had from another institution, was conferred upon him. Dr. H. C. Morrison, who is now president of the institution, presented the diploma with the following appropriate, climacteric, and congratulatory words: "Whenever and wherever I have met up and down the land a former student who has gone to school to Brother Hughes he invariably expresses gratitude that he had the high privilege of sitting under such sound instruction. Brother Hughes taught his pupils with earnestness, enthusiasm, and accuracy. He knew in his head and felt in his heart the truths which he hammered into them. He stated propositions so clearly that the students were able to grasp them." This is a great compliment to a great teacher by a great man.

CHAPTER XVIII.

AS A COLLEGE PRESIDENT.

In the founding of Asbury College, Rev. J. W. Hughes made his one noted contribution to the cause of Christian education.

History has always paid high honor and special tribute to men of initiative, foresight and inventive genius, to organizers, founders and discoverers, to the benefactors of mankind. We honor Galileo and Gutenberg for giving us the telescope and the Art of printing, we honor Christopher Columbus and John Cabot for discovering the Western Hemisphere; we honor Sir Isaac Newton for discovering the law of gravitation; we honor Sir John Mandeville or Galileo for teaching the rotundity of the earth; we honor Copernicus for teaching the rotation of the earth around the sun, known as the heliocentric system of astronomy; we honor Servetus and Dr. Harvey for the discovery of double circulation of the blood; we honor Pasteur and Virchow for teaching the germ theory; we honor Watts, Whitney, Stephenson, Fulton, Howe, Bell, Morse, Edison, Marconi, Jenner, Bloch, Selden, Rontgen, Madame Currie for their respective inventions and discoveries. We honor George Washington for founding the American nation; we praise Thomas Jefferson, the sage of Monticello, for penning the immortal Declaration of Indepen-

AS A COLLEGE PRESIDENT 197

dence; we honor Alexander Hamilton, the master builder of indissoluble union, who smote the rock of natural resources and abundant streams of revenue burst forth, who touched the corpse of public finance and it sprang upon its feet," for saving the American Constitution; we honor George Fox for founding the Society of the Friends; we honor John Wesley for founding the Methodist Church; we honor Wm. Booth for founding the Salvation Army; we honor Frances Willard for organizing the W. C. T. U.; we honor Wilbur Chapman for founding the institution of Mother's Day; we reverence Inskip, Wm. McDonald, J. A. Wood, David Updegraff and W. B. Godbey for inaugurating the modern Holiness Movement; we honor Dr. H. C. Morrison for founding The Pentecostal Herald and we honor John Wesley Hughes for founding Asbury College, the first full salvation school on the American continent.

A noted evangelist used to refer to the Pentecostal Herald and Asbury College as the two wings of the Apocalyptic Angel of the Holiness Movement. Some men found colleges or institutions of learning of which they never become presidents. John Harvard for instance, founded Harvard College but was never its president. Henry Dunster was the first president of Harvard. Moody founded the Northfield institution but never acted as its president. Many men have become presidents of colleges and universities which they never founded. But J. W. Hughes was father, founder, first president and foremost theological teacher of Asubry College. In one of the chapters of this volume he has given the history of the origin of the Institution. We believe beyond the shadow of a doubt, that he was divinely guided and providentially led in the establishment of the College. He saw the great need of such an institution; he prayed over the matter; he was impressed to launch out, to make the attempt, to begin the enterprise; he struck the old Methodist trail blazed out by Bishop Asbury one hundred years previous. He cast the die, crossed the Rubicon and came to Wilmore which at that time consisted of only three or four houses, The John Scott Place, Bob Scott's house, a log barn owned by a beef club, several cabins near the big spring, used during slave times for negroes, Dodd's store and the depot which was an inverted box car on posts.

Mr. Tom Barr, one of Wilmore's leading citizens, who was only a boy when Bro. Hughes came to Wilmore to select a location for his school, describes how on a certain day he saw a stranger, with a long Prince Albert coat on, tall and active, stepping high over the hemp field, surveying the situation. The stranger turned out to be the man of providence destined and ordained to found the famous Asbury College. Some colleges are founded by the sovereign power of the State; some by the authority of the Church; some by special booms, committees and companies; but Asbury was founded by a lone man led on by the guiding star

AS A COLLEGE PRESIDENT 199

of destiny. Like John The Baptist, who came in the spirit of Elijah, Dr. John W. Hughes came in the spirit of Bishop Asbury, who crossed the Alleghany Mountains sixty times, and was in the saddle more than Napoleon Bonaparte.

Under the active and efficient leadership of the long administration of Francis Asbury the Methodist Church in America grew from 316 to 214,000. This preeminent pioneer of early American Methodism presents a picturesque view as he rides over the rugged mountains, fords swollen streams, penetrates trackless forests, and furnishes the gospel to the first settler on the frontiers of the nation. He was "the prophet of the long road" and the most distinguished Knight of the saddle bags. He did more than any other man for the spread of Methodism over the American continent. In 1790, two years before Kentucky was admitted into the Union, he founded the first Methodist institution of learning West of the Alleghenies. He named it Bethel Academy. For lack of means and material it finally failed.

Ezra S. Tipple, author of "The Prophet of the Long Road," compliments Francis Asbury as follows: —"He comforted myriads in their sorrow and agonies, and like a tender faithful shepherd sought for lost sheep from New Hampshire to the Southern Sea, and from the Atlantic to the Blue Grass land of Kentucky. This man without a home who traveled the Long Road for a half century, and prayed in ten thousand households and preached seventeen thousand sermons, and won multitudes to Christ, made a contribution second to no other man in the creation and development of right national ideas of patriotism and religion in the new republic. If any man deserves a place in the Nation's Hall of Fame, it is Francis Asbury, the 'Prophet of the Long Road.' Again he says:—"It was by his efforts that the foundations of our educational system were laid, and he it was more than any other of his time helped to fashion the spirit and purpose of our denominational schools." In 1817 Dr. Samuel Jennings, assisted by others, opened in Baltimore, Md., an institution called Asbury College, but being without endowment it soon ceased. In 1823 Augusta College in the Northern part of Kentucky on the Ohio river was established under the presidency of Rev. J. P. Findley. In 1826, Dr. Ruter accepted the presidency. For many years it accomplished great good in the church. Among the prominent men who were educated within its walls were Bishop Foster, Prof. John Miley, the most noted teacher of Drew Seminary. The immortal Bishop Bascomb was for a time president of the College. In 1844 an attempt was made to merge it into the Transylvania University of Lexington, Ky. Augusta College ceased to exist and Transylvania University was bought by the Disciples or the Christian Church.

The Indiana Conference in 1837 established a school at Greencastle, Ind., and named it Indiana Asbury University. Later its name was changed to DePau University in honor of W. C. DePau who donated a million and half dollars to the institution.

Another Methodist College was organized at Millersburg, Ky. It was named for Wesley instead of Asbury. It is now located at Winchester, Ky., and is known as the Kentucky Wesleyan College.

The first Methodist College on the American Continent was founded by Coke and Asbury twenty miles from Baltimore on the Philadelphia road at Abingdon. It flourished for a few years but was destroyed by fire. It was re-opened in Baltimore under favorable circumstances, but in one short year it also was consumed by fire. Bishop Asbury and the friends, generally were discouraged, and abandoned the enterprise. The object of this college, which was named Cokesbury, in honor of Bishop Coke, was threefold: "First, to provide for the education of the sons of ministers, secondly, for the education and support of poor orphans; and last but not least, the establishment of a seminary for the children of our friends, where learning and religion may go hand in hand. McKendree College was founded at Lebanon, Ill., in 1825 by Peter Cartwright on a tract of land given to Bishop McKendree for valiant service rendered during the Revolutionary War.

It seems strange that during all these years, with all these different institutions, academies, colleges and universities, there was no permanant one named in honor of Bishop Asbury, the foremost maker of American Methodism, the man who stood alone during the stormy days of the Revolutionary War, when all the other Methodist ministers left and returned to England. But God moves in a mysterious way His wonders to perform. Just one hundred years after Asbury founded Bethel Academy on the banks of the Kentucky River, God inspired a man to gather up the broken threads of American Methodist history, and to restore the "Waste places" of the western wilderness, to build up Bethel from the dust according to the original ideals and plans of the heroic Asbury. So Rev. John W. Hughes, rising in his rugged strength from the hoary hills of Sweet Owen, following the star of divine providential guidance went to Wilmore, Ky., almost within a stone's throw of Bethel's ruins, where the good bishop a century before had dreamed of an institution where "Learning and religion should go hand in hand." A rock from the Old Academy was carried and put in the cornerstone of Asbury College. The institution, thus founded and established by Dr. Hughes, is the logical and legitimate successor of Bethel, the first Methodist institution of learning west of the Allegheny Mountains and second in the United States of America.

Dr. H. C. Morrison, now president of greater Asbury College, said in a recent issue of The Pentecostal Herald: "Asbury College is Wesleyan to the core. Near the spot on which it stands, the sainted Asbury held an annual conference, sent forth a little company of earnest, fearless souls to preach a full salvation in Christ. Near the site on which the College stands he built Bethel Academy, the first Methodist School in all this region, of which

Asbury College is a true successor in spirit and purpose." In view of the foregoing facts, we do not hesitate to say that Asbury College is the most fortunately, felicitously, historically, and methodistically named institution in the United States.

Dr. J. W. Hughes in founding and establishing Asbury College, has forever immortalized himself. No modern Americus Vespucci can pluck with plagiaristic hand the crown of honor from the brow of Bro. Hughes. The records of the history of the institution will recount no rival claims. The honor accorded to uncontested authors, inventors, discoverers, and founders is inviolable. The fame of the founder of a worthy institution is fixed forever. Asbury, in the onward march of its history, may have many presidents and teachers, but it can only have one founder. In the confirmation of this principle of singularity, preeminence and priority, St. Paul said to the Corinthians: "For though ye have ten thousand instructors in Christ, yet have ye not many fathers: for in Christ Jesus I have begotten you through the gospel." (Cor. 4 : 15.)

The founder of a literary institution is like the inventor of a valuable instrument or useful machine. It does not matter how much any particular invention may be modified, improved or extended, the fact remains that the inventor made it. Edison, for instance, invented the electric light. The light may be improved from time to time, yet the priority of the invention can never pale nor pass to a second place of importance. Wesley was the founder of

Methodism. The church in his day was quite small compared to the millions in the Methodist churches at the present time; yet the fact remains that Wesley is the famous founder and father of the far-flung Methodist family. Asbury College, as the years roll on, may continue to grow until it becomes a great University with thousands of students crossing its campus and crowding its classic halls. We would like to see it assume such magnificient proportions, provided it stays true to its trust, to its traditions and to the original purpose for which it was called into existence. But to whatever extent it may be enlarged, built up, beautified and equipped, the fact remains that the indefatigable John W. Hughes was its founder and first promoter. He instituted, started and established it. Yea, it was his own personal and private property for the first fifteen years of its existence.

Let no one suppose that Asbury College was a small, obscure, insignificant institution, unknown, unstandardized, and unestablished, while it was under the executive control and presidential management of Dr. Hughes. "From the very first," says Dr. H. C. Morrison, "this school has been a center of revival power and spiritual life. Out from its halls have gone hundreds of consecrated pastors, zealous evangelists and devout missionaries." Read carefully the following testimony of Dr. R. N. Rice, great scholar, teacher and historian, concerning the literary standard and collegiate work of the institution as far back as the Commencement of 1903.

"Some time since I was invited by the Rev. J. W. Hughes, president of Asbury College, Wilmore, Ky., to deliver at the commencement of that institution the annual literary address. I had looked upon it as one of the small colleges, and expected to see the day of small things. But there was a dignity and grandeur about the whole affair that I had not expected to find.

"On the night of May 22, the primary department exhibited. The large hall, capable, perhaps, of seating seven hundred people, was crowded with well-dressed and happy looking people, young and old. The exercises, presided over by Mrs. Hughes (who is at home before an audience), were a romping success.

"*There was one feature about the commencement exercises that I have never seen before. They were interspersed with revival work throughout.* There were two sermons on Saturday, three on Sunday, and one each day afterward. The afternoons were given to pentecostal services; and they were attended with power, and a number of conversions and sanctifications were reported   I preached on Saturday, and the Rev. George Asbury McLaughlin, chief editor of "The Witness," Chicago, preached every day except Saturday, and his sermons were of high order. I was especially pleased with the sermon of the Rev. H. G. Scudday. It was compact and logical as a demonstration in Euclid.

"The literary and spiritual atmosphere is excellent. The recitations, orations, dialogues, impersonations, and the music,—embracing the serious and the comic—gave great satisfaction, and came up to anything I have ever heard at the commencement of any college in an experience of over half a century. The exhibition gave evidence of thorough teaching, and very careful training for the occasion.

"I had expected to find long faces and sour godliness; but the holiness brethren are jolly souls that can laugh at a joke and shout at a sermon. I had interspersed my lecture with a number of anecdotes, which I intended to suppress if the brethren were such as did not know how to smile; after witnessing the first exhibition I determined to bring them all out; and I did, and the experiment convinced me that—

'Religion never was designed
To make our pleasures less.'

"The school is especially a nursery for young preachers, who evangelize in the summer months. Brother and Sister Hughes are doing an excellent work."

In keeping with this high encomium of Dr. Rice is the polished and appreciative paragraph of Rev. J. L. Clark, D. D., Secretary of the Kentucky Conference, which is as follows:

Asbury College was founded by the Rev. J. W. Hughes, in 1890. During the past quarter of a century this institution has made a more extensive contribution to Methodism than any other school within the bounds of the Kentucky Conference. Hundreds of ministers and scores of missionaries have received their educational equipment at Asbury College. Its student body has been composed of young men and women from many states, and from time to time various foreign countries have been represented. More foreign students are being educated at Asbury than any other college or university in the State. In recent years no institution, under Methodist management, has sent forth more foreign missionaries. Asbury has made an educational and spiritual contribution to many Conferences of both Methodisms in the United States, and scores of its alumni are preaching the Gospel of Christ to the perishing multitudes in many foreign mission fields. This institution has made inestimable contribution to Methodism at home and abroad."

We have thus far in the present chapter viewed and reviewed Dr. Hughes as the highly favored founder of Asbury College. In the other chapters in this volume we have considered him respectively as a man, as a pastor and as a theological teacher. We come now to consider him in the capacity of a college president. Was he qualified and equipped as a competent college president? Aside from all partialities of friendship, panegyric and eulogy, as a true historian, we must answer this question in the affirmative. For twenty-five years, fifteen at Asbury and ten at Kingswood, he made a splendid record as an able, competent and efficient college president. His presidential qualities and characteristics may be summed up as follows:

1. *TACT*. He was gifted with a good degree of tact. We consider this a very essential quality in the general make-up of a successful college president. Tact is knack, nice perception, skill, diplomacy, wisdom, common sense. While Dr. Hughes was tactful, yet he did not play to the gallery, cater to the crowd, or compromise with the world. He would not sacrifice principle for anyone or anything. In dealing with boys from the North and the South he knew how to avoid prejudice, and political strife and sectional discord. He would never let the students know his politics. He put principle first, the man next, and politics last. They all knew, however, that he was a full-fledged, out and out prohibitionist. He was not like the teacher from Ohio who went to Texas and revived the old war spirit of North and South, Federal and Confederate, Union and Secession. He had too much tact, skill and diplomacy to say anything that would cause pupils to divert their minds from the great essentials of salvation to party strife and political prejudice. We see the evidence of this same tactful spirit in his introductory speech at a Massachusetts camp meeting. He began his sermon to the staid New England Congregation as follows: "The first time I ever saw you blue-coats (during the war,) I thought all of you ought to have your throats cut and that I ought to help do it; but since I got full salvation, I have never known the blue from the gray. There is no Mason and Dixon line with me." The first part of his sentence shocked them, but the latter part reassured and won them.

AS A COLLEGE PRESIDENT

He knew how to meet, mix, and mingle with men. He had tact enough to run the school without trying to run the town at the same time, although he assisted in every good enterprise the town ever attempted.

2. *VERSATILITY.* He was not only armed and qualified with unfailing tact but with great versatility. Variety is the spice of life. Versatility is the power or ability to turn easily from one pursuit to another as the essence and genius of resourcefulness; it is the sure safeguard against the narrow, contracted, monotony of humdrums and hobbyists. While Dr. Hughes was a specialist, he never harped on one string. He was not a "Jack at all trades and good at none." He knew how to do several things, and do them well. He could direct, execute, manage, administer, teach, and preach. He could shift gears, change from one pursuit to another with great rapidity and rare success. He could go from the "pots and skillets" in the culinary department to the president's office, from the president's office to the chapel service; from the chapel service to the administration of discipline; and from the administration of discipline to the class room and there expound the deep doctrinal texts of theology or the philosophical dogmas of metaphysics. He was like the old fashioned general merchandise store stocked with many kinds of goods. Rev. W. D. Akers, one of his able and efficient teachers, testifies to the value, utility and variety of Dr. Hughes' famous chapel talks. He states that during the years

he was connected with the institution as a teacher, he never once heard Dr. Hughes repeat himself in his chapel talks. They were always new, soul-stirring, stimulating, and instructive. It takes more than an ordinary man to accomplish a feat like this.

3. *DEVOTION* to the pupils under his care. There is naturally a certain kind of attachment between the attorney and his client; between the employer and the employees; between the teacher and his pupils. But it seems that Dr. Hughes displayed an unusual devotion to his pupils. He showed a true, sincere father's interest in all the student body. In fact he called them his "boys" and "girls". As the Apostle Paul looked on his own converts as his special crown of joy, so Dr. Hughes regarded his students as his greatest investment toward the advancement of the cause of Christ and the extension of the Kingdom of God in the world. His highest ambition, his greatest hope was wrapped up in the personnel of his pupils. His deep devotion for them, sanctified as it were by the grace of God, caused him to dedicate all his redeemed faculties and ransomed powers for their intellectual improvement, social betterment and spiritual welfare. Hence his relationship toward them was not cold, formal, and official, but pure, lofty, solicitous, personal and paternal.

4. *FIDELITY* to the institution. In addition to his pure personal solicitude for the general welfare of the students, Dr. Hughes, deep down in his soul, maintained a deathless fidelity to the institu-

tion itself. Asbury College is the providential child of his fondest hopes, fervent prayers, and golden dreams. The bishop practically promised to give him one of the best appointments in the bounds of the conference if he would abandon the college. He not only ignored this flattering invitation, but left the far-reaching and fertile fields of evangelism which beckoned him with all their attractive and inviting charms, in order to follow the one clear clarion call to college work.

Is it any wonder that he loves as his own life the very name of Asbury College? Washington is known as the father of his country. Think of all the love, kindness, patriotism and concern concentrated in his famous farewell speech to the country he fathered and founded. Doubtless Dr. Hughes looks upon Asbury College in a somewhat similar way that Washington looked upon the land of the new republic. The college, we trust, will never forget to reverence and honor its founder.

5. *EXECUTIVE ability or administrative power*. No man is competent to be the president of a nation or an institution unless he has a sufficient degree of executive ability or administrative power. The dauntless and indomintable John Wesley Hughes was not wanting in this regard. He possessed plenty of executive power. He was not pompous and proud, neither was he arbitrary, tyrannical nor dictatorial; but he "bossed the job," and let the students know that he was the head of the executive department of the collegiate institution. He held the high hand

of authority over the college constituency. All was not peaceful, at all times, on the Potomac. There were wars, insurrections, rebellions and bolshevistic invasions, nevertheless and notwithstanding the old "Ship of State" was steered through the stormy seas to a safe harbor. The holiness people are naturally and constitutionally hard to govern. The reason of this is found in the fact that they have to make a regular declaration of independence in order to receive the experience of full salvation. They throw off many restraints and restrictions. They feel free and independent. They obey God rather than man. The baptism with the Spirit develops individuality and personality. Hence the holiness people do not come at every nod and beck of ecclesiastical authority. But in standing so straight there is danger of leaning backward. So it must not be supposed that a holiness institution can be run without a hitch or "switch." Dr. Hughes, in the early stages of Asbury College, met this very problem. Those who stood off and threw stones at him were in no position to appreciate the situation. Dr. Hughes never professed to be above faults, mistakes, errors and infirmities. But in spite of all he plowed through to victory and success. He was frank, sincere, honest, desperately in earnest, energetic, and enthusiastic. During the early days of the institution there were gathered within the college walls every type and stripe and characteristic of student life, good, bad, and indifferent. Some were studious and obedient, others were as green as gourds, rough as pig-iron, and as wild as Rocky Mountain goats. The president had a man's job to manage all these heterogeneous elements of his constituency. He had to have the tact of the teacher, the diplomacy of the statesman, the strategy of the general, the shrewdness of the lawyer and the impartiality of the judge.

Dr. Hughes was not a mere nominal, formal, absentee, proxy president. He was a real actual residential president. He defended the "constitution" and faithfully executed the office of college president.

6. *THE ABILITY* to select a first class faculty. An all-round college president must have the skill to select a competent corps of college teachers. If he fails at this vital point he is weighed in the balances and found wanting. Dr. Hughes was fortunate in securing a fine faculty. He gathered together an excellent group of superior teachers in every department of college work. His rule was to secure as instructors in the institution men and women of high intellectual attainments, good moral character, and deep spirituality. To fancy that he had an inferior faculty was far-fetched. A hasty review of some of his star teachers will show how well he succeeded in the selection of a fine faculty.

7. *SPEAKERS EMPLOYED*. The ability to select and employ proper and prominent speakers is another test of the caliber and capacity of a college president. Dr. Hughes was an adept in this respect. Among the leading holiness representatives

which he brought to the college platform from time to time, thus giving the students the benefit of their rare gifts and rich experiences were Dr. C. J. Fowler, president of the National Holiness Association; Dr. E. F. Walker, great theologian, at one time moderator of the Indianapolis Presbytery; Dr. G. A. McLaughlin, Editor or the Christian Witness; Rev. Joseph H. Smith, great teacher and evangelist; B. Carradine, eminent author and evangelist; and Isaiah Reid, a strong writer and clear advocate of full salvation. Great social reformers with their respective messages were sought and brought upon the platform such as Dr. Wilbur F. Crafts, Susan B. Anthony, Mary Lathrop, known as the Daniel Webster of the W. C. T. U., and the immortal inhibitive Carrie Nation. Other noted speakers and preachers included Dr. M. Parkhurst, the great Bible exegete, who for nine years conducted the Lexington Chautauqua, the heroic Bishop Lambuth, Bishop H. C. Morrison, J. C. C. Newton, Japan, Miss Belle H. Bennett, prominent Home Missionary worker of the M. E. Church, S., Dr. R. N. Rice, star of the first magnitude in the Holston Conference, and Dr. Alexander Redd, one of the most intellectual men in the Kentucky Conference and Dr. Gross Alexander.

Let us finally in conclusion conservatively say that John Wesley Hughes, during the twenty-five years he served in the capacity of college president, rendered valuable, faithful, efficient, and far-reaching service, and deserves the plaudit "well done."

ANDREW JOHNSON.

CHAPTER XIX.

HOLINESS CAMP MEETINGS.

Thirty years ago last August Dr. H. C. Morrison and myself were walking down by the grounds known now as the Central Holiness Camp Grounds. While in busy conversation I called his attention to what is now the camp ground, a nice woodland, and said to him: "At no distant date I mean to have a full salvation camp meeting on those grounds." He replied: "Good for you! That is a fine idea."

I prayed earnestly about the matter and after much prayer and consultation with Rev. C. M. Humphrey and J. A. Sawyer, members of the Kentucky Conference of the Methodist Episcopal Church, South, we sent for a tent and held our first camp meeting, which was a splendid success. Many souls were saved and sanctified, and the saints of God were encouraged to back the project. My objective was to so connect the college and the camp meeting as to make them mutual supports.

At the close of the camp meeting I aimed to raise one thousand dollars and succeeded in raising eleven hundred, which built the present auditorium. When I began the collection a friend of mine said he thought I could not get more than three hundred dollars out of that crowd. But we of the holiness ranks know something of the giving proclivities of the holiness people who are bent on spreading Scriptural Holiness. We put on the building the motto, "HOLINESS UNTO THE LORD;" the promotion of which means its final success, the neglect of which means its final failure. The objective of Asbury College and Central Holiness Camp Meeting must be fully carried out to please God, who put them on my heart, and I have felt from the beginning that if either or both should ever reach the day in their history when this was not their objective, God would have no more use for them and they would die a natural death.

One of the most efficient agencies in the promotion of the holiness revival throughout the country is the Holiness Camp Meeting, where hungry people, who do not get the full Gospel at their homes, can come and be fed; the unsaved and unsanctified can get saved and wholly sanctified; and the ministers of the Gospel who need to hear somebody else preach, and get refreshed and refired, bringing their flocks and putting them in touch with full- salvation camp meetings; where, thanks to God, tens of thousands have been saved, sanctified and established in the great doctrine and experiences of full salvation, and so instructed by capable leaders and speakers as to keep them from backsliding, or falling into some phase of "extremism" or fanaticism, such as the third blessing, gift of tongues, and other perversions by the enemy of souls.

A number of years ago a gentleman asked me when I was going to have my Kingswood camp meeting, saying his wife recently had obtained the blessing of holiness, and he was a seeker of the blessing himself. I had as usual a great preacher leading the meeting that year. A minister friend of mine, a graduate of a great theological seminary, heard the interview and said to the gentleman: "You will get more information in a ten days' holiness camp meeting on the subject of salvation and especially of holiness, than you will get in the usual theological seminary in a year." I positively know that that is not an exaggeration for I know by experience and observation that it is correct. It grieved me from my heart to have to endorse such a statement, notwithstanding it is true. Dr. E. F. Walker, then of the Presbyterian Church, one of the greatest preachers it has been my privilege to know in or out of the Holiness Movement, said to a class of graduates in Asbury College while I was president: "Young ladies and gentlemen, over in California where I received my theological education, the president said to our class entering the course, 'When our boys are beginners they are spiritual; when middlers they are backsliders; when seniors they are reprobates.'" I would not infer from this statement that such conditions obtained universally in theological seminaries, but I am of the opinion, after long observation, that it is lamentably true in many instances, and that an honest inquirer after the fundamental teachings of the Holy Scriptures gets his mind confused, his faith stunned and often destroyed.

I believe a young man with a well trained mind,

and a heart full of the love of God, with a divine call to the ministry, could not do better than to make it his custom annually to put himself in contact with the teachings, and fire-baptized testimonies and fellowships that are found in full salvation camp meetings, which he cannot find in other educational and religious assemblies. I am also sure that the congregation cannot make a better investment, if they want the old-time fire on their preacher and themselves, so as to keep a revival running the year around, than to make it a point not only to go themselves once a year to such a meeting, but do all in their power to get their pastor in contact with such a meeting by seeing that his expenses are all met, and that he be excused from his pulpit on Sunday.

After a careful study of the greatest problem of the church and the ministry, namely, how to get men to God, I do not hesitate to say that no movement of the people of God has counted more for the time and money invested, than the camp meeting movement.

I entered the ministry forty-seven years ago in the Kentucky Conference, Methodist Episcopal Church, South, of course, as an inexperienced young man; and big men in the church seemed larger than they do now. I heard two of them talking one day, both being ministers. One said to the other: "The day of revivals, old-fashioned class meetings, and consequent emotional display has passed. Nobody but the illiterate whites and the negroes have them any more." I knew that I was not a negro, and I also knew that I was not a literary white, but deep down in my soul, the Holy Spirit so stirred my heart with righteous indignation and bull-dog determination that I vowed, "Those times shall come back again, so far as I am concerned." I have always thanked God that the conference had good men that did possess and teach clear-cut salvation and urged young preachers to contend for the old-time revivals. The one who had much to do with my pressing the work when a young man, was my *big brother*, Dr. E. L. Southgate, who has been my constant counsellor through life. Peace be to his closing days and memory when he shall have gone, and also to my old college mate, Dr. Alexander Redd, my life companion and never failing friend, whose great heart, head and counsel have meant much to me, both members of my Conference.

It took our conference at least ten years to get a correct vision of the scripturalness and desirability of an old-fashioned, second-of-Acts, Apostolic, Wesleyan revival. We are told in Methodist history that Mr. Wesley and George Whitefield, and their coadjutors preached to tens of thousands in the open air; that Mr. Whitefield was known to preach to a hundred thousand people on the commons, and had ten thousand people saved under one sermon. Bishop Asbury, the Wesley of America, underwent the privation of separating from his mother when a young man, the privations of being without family life, and the privation of having no home, spending and being spent, getting men saved and sanctified, and acting as a great superintendent of the most widespread revivals among his preachers and people, that this country has ever known, which continue to spread and will no doubt until time shall be no more. We, their lineal ecclesiastical successors, owe it to God, to ourselves, to our fellowmen to project and press every salvation movement that our God honored, predecessors projected before we came on the scene of life. Shame on the Methodists, and especially the Methodist preachers, who would in the smallest way insinuate against, or interfere with, the typical old Methodist revivals and camp meetings! Better for them if they had not been born. There is no way to promote full salvation that ignores genuine revivals; and no way to preserve the fundamentals of the Holy Scriptures, except through the baptism with the Holy Spirit, which is always instrumental in **promoting** revivals of religion.

Central Holiness Camp Ground, and the Kingswood Camp Meeting, which God permitted me to project in 1906 in connection with Kingswood College, have been the instruments in the hand of God of introducing full salvation to thousands of people who possibly would not otherwise have heard of it. I was so thoroughly occupied the year that I started Kingswood College, that it was suggested to me that I omit the camp meeting that year. But I built a brush arbor, and employed Revs. A. A. Niles, of the Baptist church, and J. M. Pike, editor of the "Way of Faith," and held our first camp meeting with one hundred and fifty people saved or sanctified. For the last seventeen years it has made no uncertain sound on full salvation lines. In connection with the camp meeting and college and workers sent out from both, I feel safe in saying that within a radius of thirty miles three thousand souls have been led to God.

Long live these college adjuncts and soul winning centers! They are almost as sacred to me as my relation to God. For I believe God allows me to say modestly and religiously that they cost me some of the hardest struggles, and were the most profitable efforts of my life. No thoughtful, serious person criticizes a parent for trying to protect his own child. So, when I speak of these joint projects of Wilmore and Kingswood, I think I may be excused for saying with Paul, in referring to his fatherly sympathy and love for those he had begotten in the Lord: "Ye may have many teachers, but one father."

CHAPTER XX.

MARY WALLINGFORD HUGHES.

In giving a sketch of my life I feel it would be entirely incomplete not to give some account of the woman who has made my life and work worth while.

The twenty-eighth day of July, 1881, we were married. She was a vigorous, high-life leader of the young people with whom she associated. While in the church, like the majority of young people, she was not spiritual, and took an active part in all young people's amusements. Reared in a community with a peculiar combination of teachings on religious lines—one class of teachers emphasizing the human to the neglect of the divine, an opposite class emphasizing the divine to the neglect of the human, she became confused as to her belief on the subject of real orthodoxy. Of course, her experience was at sea on religious lines, having really no spiritual experience. Of course, the mean between two extremes she had not met at all and was a stranger to Arminian Methodism. She had joined the Methodist church in a mere protracted meeting where they did not teach the absolute necessity of the new birth, and knew nothing of the supernatural birth, or other fundamentals of salvation. I knew when I was visiting her that she was not a saved woman and I went on my knees before God and told Him that unless He gave me the assurance that she would become a Christian an cooperate with me in salvation work of the ministry I would not press my suit any further. I got an unequivocal answer from God assuring me that the work would be done. I settled the question then that my affections had not been misplaced, for the first time I saw her I said of all women I have ever seen she is to me the most attractive, and unless I feel different toward her after further acquaintance I shall ask her to be my life companion. The more I saw of her the more I was convinced that she was the woman that I wanted for my wife, and it gives me pleasure to say that there was never a moment before or after marriage that I had reason to change my mind.

During our courtship I did what I believed ought to be done in all prospective matrimonial alliances, for the most momentous of all matters save the salvation of souls is the marital relations, which should be seriously, prayerfully, and thoughtfully weighed before entered into. I put the subject of salvation with its gravity and the responsibility of the ministry before her with perfect candor as far as I knew how, before we were joined together in the holy estate of matrimony, so that she would have no reason to regret taking this serious step with a man whom she had known but a few months. I felt absolutely certain that she took in all that I said with perfect seriousness and honesty and would be willing to meet the issues that would probably come in the life of a minister's wife.

When we began life together she became an honest inquirer into the teachings of the Bible and the great doctrines and experiences of salvation. Seventeen months of that time she was a very earnest seeker and honest inquirer through all possible human and divine sources to discover and realize the full teachings of the Bible and experience of a "know-so salvation. In 1882 in Chaplin Methodist Church, Nelson County, Kentucky, in a meeting in which I was assisted by Dr. W. B. Godbey, she was gloriously converted at an altar of prayer while praying in an audible voice. I heard her when she left the penitent side of life, laid hold of God by faith and received a sweet assurance of real salvation. The utterance that she made at this time was "Abba Father" (my Father) with a quivering voice and joyful accentuation. I went to her at once, put my hand in hers and asked her to look me in the face. When she did, I said, "What have you?" She replied, "I am happier than I have ever been before in my life. My soul is satisfied." I said, "That is salvation."

Her salvation was so clear and satisfactory to herself and to all who knew her, she at once became a great instrument in the salvation of others, being the means of the salvation of her mother and most of her family. She arose from that altar and began at once to assist me at the altar and became, I believe, the most efficient and fruitful altar assistant with whom I ever labored. She evidently had a special gift from God for

MARY WALLINGFORD HUGHES

that wonderful work. Of all the sciences in the world, to my mind, the science of leading souls to God is the highest. For thirty-three years, four months and eight days we traveled life's way together. She never wavered either in her experience or in her work for God. When everything else would become stale, as often will be the case in varied experiences of family life, it was one of the common things for this remark to be passed from one to the other: "The religion of Jesus Christ never ceases to interest us." Sick or well, home or abroad, in the severest of financial tests, when the death angel came into the home, which occurred four times in our family of children, even then we were able not only to stand and see the loved ones pass away, but talk over the dead body warning others to get ready to meet God.

In the little town of Wilmore when our third child, four years of age, slipped away to God, she stood over his dead body and warned others to get ready to meet God. There was a man in the church that day who had not been in church for nine years, assigned as his reason for being there that day that he heard that the holiness people did not cry and demonstrate over their dead as did other people. The service so impressed him that he went away from the church, saying, "I don't understand how people think as they seem to." Human nature is the same everywhere. The sanctifying grace of God alone answers this question. She was sanctified in Asbury College chapel, Commencement, 1892.

As a Christian, I never saw her surpassed; as a counsellor, always safe. Nothing seemed to excite her. When the college caught on fire during chapel service one morning, she did her utmost in common with others, but without any indications of excitement. She practiced rigid economy with herself and family. She was a loving, painstaking, indulgent mother. She was a true wife and co-worker in the pastorate, in revivals and evangelistic work. She was the mother, not only of eight children, but a mother of two colleges and a godmother to many hundreds of other sons and daughters.

She was beautiful in person, winsome in manners, faultless in conduct, honest to the core, absolutely trustworthy, constant in affection, mentally alert, well furnished, thoughtful of others, self-poised, at home in all social circles, self sacrificing, always glad to aid others, liberal to a fault, abundant in labors, a born leader in all church and W. C. T. U. work, having organized the W. C. T. U. at Wilmore, Kentucky and for a long time its president. No vital issue, either on moral or religious lines, failed to get her earnest attention and solid support. She was an extraordinary trainer of children on all lines of literary, missionary and Sunday School entertainments. Among the sick, everybody's friend; a mother of students, administering to body, mind and soul. *It may be truly said that she gave herself for others.*

The strenuousness of college life with her home

duties and financial pressure and other perplexing problems to solve became too severe for her overworked constitution and for a number of years before she went away she began to have severe attacks of pulmonary trouble. For a number of winters I took her South which always seemed to rejuvenate her and help her to get along until the next winter. Finally the time came when she made up her mind that she would not go South and despite all the arguments that I could bring to bear upon her she would not consent to go. The severity of that winter was too much for her, and she never recovered from the backset. Very few people who knew her were aware of what a strong will she had with her splendid mental balance and quietness. When she believed that she was right she held on to her determination as her life motto. For almost two years she lived beyond what the doctors who examined her, said that she could live. I have always felt that she did it by her determination and faith in God. The time was approaching when the machinery must give way so I went to the doctors one day and said, "Gentlemen, as far as I can see, my wife is going away soon." They said, "You are correct about it." I interviewed her that day, telling her the situation. She talked as calmly about it as if she were about to take an ordinary journey. And when the end came and the last goodbye had been said, she looked up and said, "I am going to heaven, I am going to heaven," and was translated that moment from her fragile frame to the City of God on high. I do not hesitate to say she lived a life more divine than human, because she was guided constantly by His Holy Spirit. And it may be truly said of her, "She fought a good fight and kept the faith." If my life has been worth anything to the world she was largely responsible for it, and if I should be called by any of my friends, "The father of Asbury and Kingswood Colleges," she ought to be called "The mother". This thought was expressed at her funeral by Andrew Johnson in the following eulogy:

"We honor Susanna Wesley as the Mother of Methodism; we honor Katherine Booth as the Mother of the Salvation Army; we honor Mary Hughes as the Mother of Holiness Colleges. As a student of Asbury College I was blessed and benefited by her motherly council and calm consecrated Christian conduct."

CHAPTER XXI.

GREATER ASBURY.

Educational institutions are in many ways similar in their origin, growth and development to the growth and development of human life, with its fears within and fightings without. There are days of normal growth; seasons and times of refreshing and encouragement and times of depression and discouragement. Especially is this true of full-salvation schools. The devil and his followers have one objective, and God and His followers have another very different one.

The school in which I spent some time, in one of our literary societies, we had the following motto: "Mens est vir," (The mind is the man). This is only partially true and leads to merely intellectual culture for which the devil and sinful men invest themselves and their means; for the more intelligence a man possesses, the more capable he is for carrying out Satan's plans in the destruction of mankind. Sir Wm. Hamilton, among the greatest of philosophers, endorsed this view when he said, "There is nothing great in the universe but man, and nothing great in man but mind," which represents very largely the educational world, which is false and lop-sided education, always resulting in rationalism. The Greeks and Romans laid constant emphasis on this phase of education, which, unfortunately, the Christian Church has largely endorsed and practiced. Christianity alone changed this view, stressing the moral and religious culture of man. All real Christian schools insist upon the motto: "Psyche esti anthropos." (The soul is the man.) For the mind is only a faculty of the soul made in the moral and spiritual image of God, and all education is incorrect that does not teach that the soul must be brought into vital connection with God and His laws. All secular schools, and many, I am sorry to say, church schools, having overlooked this all-important question in Christian education have brought about the necessity of pronounced full-salvation schools in which the soul is developed in common with the mind and body.

Asbury College, the first holiness or full-salvation college in this country, would never have been in existence had the church schools done their full duty at this long neglected and essential point in real Christian education. (These individual and independent, interdenominational schools never would have been in existence but for the above facts.) I wish from my heart of hearts that the time would soon come when the church schools would take up this line of work. Then the necessity of independent, interdenominational schools would cease to be necessary. Unless they do it, the full-salvation schools are an absolute necessity and no doubt will continue to multiply and enlarge; for there are men and women, Spirit-filled and Spirit-led who will put their thought, prayers, influence and money into schools that contend for the faith once delivered to the saints; where they hope to get their sons and daughters under first-class educational environment with such spiritual influences as will get them saved and sanctified, and fully prepared for life's work. The average school ignores and often viciously repudiates the teaching that leads young life into a strictly moral and spiritual life based on the doctrines and experiences taught in the Bible and by our Holy Christianity. Contrariwise they seem to take a delight in destroying the faith of the youth in the great fundamental teachings and experiences that make Christian men and women.

In the projecting and establishing of Asbury College in the fifteen years of my administration it had a normal and successful growth, and closed out with its most successful commencement. But following my administration, for several years it continued to lose ground, until the Management, as I was informed by the president of the Board, had made up their minds that unless they could secure Dr. H. C. Morrison as its president that they would close the school. When Dr. Morrison took his world tour, the last thing I said to him was, "Considering the present status of Asbury College you will have to take its presidency." For I saw clearly that that was then their only hope, and that he was the logical and only man in my judgment that could take it up in its depleted condition and put it on its feet. He was the founder and editor and owner of The Pentecost Herald, one of the best mediums of communication in the Holiness Movement, and was the logical man for the place.

As soon as he returned from the Orient a committee was sent to him. They told him that the school was in such a run-down condition that unless he did give his consent to become its president they would let it go by default. When Dr. Morrison and I met, the first thing he said to me was, "I did what you said I would have to do if Asbury College should continue its existence." I had learned by experience that any pronounced holiness, independent, interdenominational school could not be permanently established without its own medium of communication through which its work, needs and objective could be made known constantly to those who had seen and felt the absolute need of such a school, where their sons and daughters in common with other men's sons and daughters, could get a first-class education under such spiritual influences as would lead them to seek the experience of regeneration and entire sanctification and would lead them into Christian work in any avocation of life. And they would gladly patronize such a school. And those who had money to invest in religious educational enterprises would be glad to put it where it would bring the best results.

I know of no man who can do so many things well as Dr. Henry Clay Morrison. He is a peer among the best preachers in this country. He is a great religious editor as to versatility, quantity, and quality of his writings. His publishing plant is a marvelous force in distributing good books. His religious zeal, oratory and indomitable energy have put him to the front as an evangelist and soul winner. His broad vision, insight and foresight have made him a great college president. Under his wise presidency he has not only put Asbury College back on its feet, but it has grown by leaps and bounds in buildings, students, teachers, and general enlargement of the work until it has become one of the large religious institutions of the land, and possibly no school in this country of its age has sent out more ministers and missionaries than Asbury College.

The following facts will show its marvelous progress on all lines under his splendid administration. I closed my administration with one brick and six wooden buildings on a campus of fourteen and a quarter acres, estimated by the board at $40,000. (It would be near $90,000 now.) I took $25,0000 for the property with the understanding that I was to remain as president so long as I desired, giving, of course, $15,000 to the college. It now has eight brick and four wooden buildings, campus of seventeen acres, estimated at $700,000. I had fifteen teachers, about three hundred students; it now has forty teachers and over 670 students; It then had sixty-five studying for the ministry and missionary work; it now has two hundred. It then had twenty states and several foreign countries represented; it now has forty states and representatives from six foreign countries.

As Asbury grows, by the grace of God, its work will enlarge its own borders. It is supported by the believers in full salvation and as these are increased by the ministers and evangelists that go out from its walls, so will the school be perpetually enlarged.

The seminaries and many church schools are failing to meet the religious problems of today. Many eyes are turned toward Asbury, where the great imperishable and eternal truths are upheld and where competent and conservative scholarship is encouraged. If God is put first we need not fear a liberal education nor proper physical culture. It is not incredible that in twenty-five years there may be on the Asbury hill one of the most important plants and theological seminaries in America—A school uncompromisingly true to the Word of God; powerful in opposition to unorthodox thought, and so-called modern religion, and a great break-water against the infidelity and godlessness of our times.

CHAPTER XXII.

AS A PREACHER.

A divine call to the Christian ministry constitutes the first essential element in the make-up of a genuine preacher of the true gospel. The twelve members of the Apostolic College were called, commissioned, ordained and sent forth with the charge to preach, to heal the sick, cleanse the lepers, raise the dead and cast out devils. "Freely ye have received, freely give." Saul of Tarsus, the double-graduate, the arch-persecutor of the faith, on his way to Damascus saw in the heavens a light brighter than the noonday sun and heard a voice in the Hebrew, crying, "Saul ,Saul, Why persecutest thou me?" Terrified, unnerved and unhorsed he fell sprawling to the earth. Out of the dust of this catastrophe he was called into the apostleship. His commission received in this connection carried him as a minister and missionary both to the Jew and the the Gentile, bond and free, To open their eyes, to turn them from darkness to light and from the power of Satan unto God, that they may receive forgiveness of sins and inheritance among them which are sanctified by faith.

The great trouble with the Church today, there are too many self-constituted, man-made preachers filling the pulpits of the land who are not divinely called. For various reasons and through different motives they have entered the ministry. Hence, we have all kinds of preachers preaching all kinds of doctrines, dogmas, fads and theories;—Roman, Unitarian, Darwinian, New Thought, Free Thought, Modern Thought, Soap, Soup, Sunshine and Sociological Service. Many of the modern ministers sneer, ridicule and make fun of a "call to preach," thus demonstrating to the world the fact that they themselves have never received authority from the proper source to proclaim the Gospel.

God, according to the councils of His own will, calls His ministers and selects His men in His own peculiar way. He chooses them from every rank of society and from all the walks of life. In the present instance He searched out a young man, who, when sixteen years of age was unable to read and write. This same young man, like so many people of today, had united with the church without salvation. He was never satisfied with his religious status. On a certain occasion he was providentially led to attend a real old-time Holy Ghost revival where souls were praying through to victory and being soundly converted to God. He soon saw that his formal, ritualistic religion would not stand the test. He got under awful conviction and sought the Lord for several days and at last was happily and gloriously converted, receiving a know-so salvation. This revolutionized his whole career. He was now ready to enter any field of Christian service to which he might be called. But he would never consent to preach the gospel unless he was absolutely sure that he was definitely and divinely called to this sacred office. So he carried the question to God in earnest prayer and was called as clearly as if God had spoken to him in an audible voice from the sky. For over fifty years there has never been the shadow of a doubt in his mind as to his call to preach. A call to preach is a call for preparation to preach. Accordingly he went to college and studied for the ministry. He was not educated *for* the ministry but educated *in* the ministry. He tested the truth of the old saying,—the best way to learn how to preach is to preach.

All worldly aggrandizements and emoluments of office are not to be compared to the high and holy order of the Christian ministry. The preacher as a reaper of life's harvest is a plenipotentiary representative of the skies. In the highest sense of the term he has greater honor than all earthly potentates, kings, monarchs and American presidents. Hence a great responsibility rests upon the consular minister of the Most High.

All preachers, generally speaking, have some points in common yet each particular preacher has his own personality, peculiarities and characteristic features. We will now proceed to size up the ministerial calibre and character of the Reverend John Wesley Hughes.

1. *He was primarily a preacher*. We have already considered him in the biographical portion of this volume as a man, as a pastor, as a theological professor and as a college president. We will now describe him as a preacher. He was first and

foremost a preacher. While he was a good pastor, he was also a good preacher. If anything he was a better preacher than he was a pastor. In all his ministerial capacity his preaching ability was preeminent. When he became a college professor he did not cease to be a preacher. It is often the case that when a preacher becomes a theological teacher he bids farewell to his former "profession." He forgets, as it were, that he was once a preacher. He must now specialize and give all of the time to theological training. He soon gets out of the practice of preaching and loses the fiery prophetic spirit of evangelism. But this was not the case with John W. Hughes. In addition to all his collegiate work he preached more than many regular preachers. The preacher was never lost in the teacher or president. He did not blend or confuse the three distinct offices. He could teach when he sat in the theological chair and preach when he stood behind the sacred desk in the pulpit.

It is true that he taught earnestly and enthusiastically and often put more energy in his teaching than many ministers put in their sermons. Yet he did not substitute preaching for teaching. He was so imbued with the evangelistic spirit that he could drop into a revival meeting at any stage and preach a sermon without breaking the connection or effecting the morale of the meeting.

After he received the divine call to the ministry, which in his case was so definite and indubitable, he always put great emphasis upon the preaching

AS A PREACHER

of the Word. His main purpose in founding Asbury College was to train young men and women for Christian service, for the ministry and for the mission fields. In his long and useful career the preacher was always present, prominent and paramount. He was a preacher before he ever thought of founding a college; he was a preacher during his collegiate activity and he remains a preacher after the close of his college career.

Even now he does not want to be recognized as a former theological professor or as an ex-college president or president emeritus but as a plain, practical preacher of the old time gospel. This shows how he appraised and how he appreciated the highly honored avocation of the Christian ministry. In all his plans and purposes he was essentially first and last a preacher.

2. *He was, and is, a Methodist preacher.* He was converted in a Methodist revival, joined the Methodist church and entered the Methodist ministry. While he was always able to give an intelligent reason for his denominational affiliation, yet, he was not a denominational bigot, but was a friend to all evangelical churches. He believed and preached the great cardinal doctrines of Methodism, such as the free moral agency of man, the universal atonement, conditional election, conditional final perseverance of the saints or the possibility of apostasy, prevenient grace, conviction, justification by faith, regeneration, adoption, the witness of the Spirit and entire sanctification.

He was Methodistic from the standpoint of earnestness. Dr. Thomas Chalmers, the eloquent Scotch divine, declared that Methodism was Christianity in earnest. Dr. Hughes could easily qualify as a Methodist preacher on that line. The old time Methodist preacher was active, intense and always on the alert. He preached in demonstration of the Spirit and of power. Under his pointed and powerful ministry people fell at the mourner's bench and cried for mercy. Dr. Hughes has often characterized himself as an old fashioned John Wesleyan Methodist. He had the spirit, the zeal, the perfect love, the unconquerable enthusiasm and the general earmarks of the primitive Methodist preacher.

How far from the faith of the fathers have many of the modern Methodist ministers wandered! Pity the poor prodigals! They may claim that they are living in a different age now. No, we are living in the same gospel dispensational age in which Wesley lived. We are not living in the Mosaic age of the past nor in the millennial age to come, but are living in the present gospel age or the Holy Ghost dispensation. They may say that "times" have changed. Very well, God has not changed, Christ is the same, the Bible is the same, the devil is the same, sin is the same, the need of the soul is the same. The doctrines of the Holy Scriptures are exactly the same. The world is propagated in the same way. Principles are eternal. They never change. So, thou art inexcusable, O modern Methodist, who substitutes sociology for theology and the Darwinian theory of evolution for the Bible view of Divine creation!

Dr. J. W. Hughes is not a mediating modernist nor a compromising Methodist, but a true, genuine, orthodox, evangelical, old-time, historical, full-fledged, out-and-out, dyed-in-the-wool Methodist preacher. The parchment of the Methodist preacher, being the prophetic mantle of ministerial authority, is more ancient than the Golden Fleece, and more honorable than the Royal Garter, or any of the regalia or paraphernalia of earthly potentates or fraternal societies.

We have thus far considered Dr. Hughes as a preacher, primarily and paramount, and as a Methodist preacher doctrinally and denominationally. We come to another classification.

3. *He was a Holiness preacher.* Some may ask if this is not included in the Methodist category. In the multiplication and modification of Methodism it has long since come to pass that Methodist and Holiness are not necessarily synonymous terms. All Methodist preachers according to the constitution of the church, ought to be holiness preachers, but, alas, many of them are very far gone from original Methodism, and of their own free-will and accord inclined to rationalism and that continually. We call Dr. Hughes a holiness preacher within the pales of Methodism because he has been very pronounced and prominent in preaching Bible holiness or entire sanctification as a second definite, distinct work of grace. He has devoted a very interesting chapter

in the present volume to his experience of sanctification.

Since that great spiritual epoch transpired in his life he has been a strong advocate of what John Wesley called the grand depositum of Methodism. Wesley, it will be remembered, defined sanctification as an instantaneous deliverance from all sin which includes a power, then given, to always cling to God. Dr. Adam Clarke defined it as the washing of the soul of a true believer from the remains of sin, while Webster's Dictionary defines it as a work of divine grace by which the affections of men are alienated from sin and exalted to a supreme love of God.

Dr. Hughes, in the presence of friend and foe, would always testify to the experience at the Annual Conferences. He founded the college for the promotion of holiness. He also established the Central Holiness Camp Meeting at Wilmore, Kentucky, and Kingswood Camp Meeting at Kingswood, Kentucky, in order to spread scriptural holiness over the land.

In view of all these facts and circumstances he may be correctly classified as a holiness preacher, par excellent. He is glad to be counted among the number of preachers who have given the best part of their lives in propagating and proclaiming the blessed truth of full and free salvation.

4. *He is an evangelistic preacher.* There are many good preachers, good pastors and even holiness preachers who are not specially gifted as evan-

AS A PREACHER

gelists. John W. Hughes was naturally, constitutionally and spiritually gifted as an evangelist. He was quick, active, positive, decisive, daring, dashing and dynamic. He was full of fire, zeal and enthusiasm. He has a voice like thunder. His powerful, explosive, denunciatory utterances would wake up formal church members from their phlegmatic and dogmatic slumber and cause the cold chills to chase each other up and down the spinal column of the careless sinner. He was once preaching in the court house at Owenton, Kentucky, when a thunder storm arose. There came a keen flash of lightning, followed by a terrific peal of thunder. Dr. Hughes mingled the thunder and lightning of Sinai with the roar of the elements, crying out in stentorian tones—"What if the lightning should strike you dead, where would your soul go?"

Years after the incident one who was present on the occasion related the incident to the writer. He said it frightened him and made the cold chills run over him. It also convinced and made a lasting impression upon him. Many a weak-voiced preacher could not have stood the storm or stemmed the flood, but the boisterous evangelist tuned in and turned the storm to his advantage.

Dr. Hughes always insisted upon a know-so salvation. He had no use for a mere card-signing, hand-shaking, church-joining protracted meeting. He commenced with the unconverted members of the church and preached them under conviction. He emphasized the witness of the Spirit and applied the truth on this line to the formal professors of religion. They soon saw that they were not right and that it took more than mere morality and church membership to save them. When he had located them he began to preach on the terrors of the law, repentance, restitution, death, hell and judgment. An awful nightmare of conviction would settle down upon the people. The evangelist would never let up. He held the truth before the congregation. "Ye must be born again" was the slogan and battle cry of his campaign.

Sometimes the revival would start with the conversion of a prominent church member. Then the fire would spread all over the town. At other times the break would come with a spontaneous rush to the altar.

Brother Hughes knew how to rightly divide the word of truth. He had a message, not only for the unsaved, but for the Christian. He preached the doctrine of entire sanctification to believers and led many of them into the experience.

Much of his evangelistic work was done while he was a pastor in the Kentucky Conference. One of the conservative members of the conference paid Dr. Hughes the following compliment:

"I have followed him on several charges and found more additions, more conversions, more parsonages built and repaired, churches built and repaired, and benevolences paid in full in his wake than any man I ever followed."

It will be observed by all these signs and seals,

tokens and credentials of his ministry that he was an evangelistic pastor. He was a flaming evangel throughout the conference connection. Pastors called him to conduct their meetings. Success crowned his efforts. His name and fame began to spread over the country. Calls to conduct revivals came thick and fast. He finally decided to devote his entire time to evangelistic work. At the next annual conference he located and made his home and headquarters at Carlisle, Kentucky. He was now ready to swing out in the white harvest field of special evangelism. But he only spent one year in this capacity. Just as he was beginning to loom large on the horizon of special evangelistic activity, he received a clarion call to concentrate his energies to the founding of a new institution in the world.

From the human viewpoint at least, it might look like a questionable mode of procedure, if not a mistake, for this man with such marked evangelistic gifts to give up the work in which he was so eminently successful. But our limited human foresight is not as good as our hindsight. In the light of the history of Asbury College we can all now plainly see the guiding hand of Providence dealing with Dr. Hughes in those days. Like the miracle of the loaves and fishes under the multiplying touch of the Divine fingers, the usefulness of one man was increased a thousandfold. It is just like God to take us and break us and make us a blessing!

5. *He was a doctrinal preacher.* We do not mean that he was all the time harping on baptism,

close communion, falling from grace, the name of the church and apostolic succession. He had too much religion and too much common sense to waste all his time on non-essentials and small denominational differences. He was a doctrinal preacher in the sense that he proclaimed the great essential doctrines of salvation. In other words, he was a great theologian. He taught systematic theology for twenty-five years. Hence he was well posted on the great fundamental doctrines of the Bible.

The president of one of the great holiness camp meetings in Ohio recently said to the writer: "I have Brother Hughes in the camp to keep my preachers straight on theology."

ANDREW JOHNSON.

APPRECIATIONS.

A WORD OF APPRECIATION

For Rev. J. W. Hughes, D. D., former president and founder of Asbury and Kingswood Colleges.

Some fifteen years ago, while prayerfully considering where I should go and finish my college work, I was Divinely impressed to attend Kingswood College. At this place I came in contact with Dr. J. W. Hughes, and his dear precious wife who have meant as much to me as any other persons in the world. They helped to put the old-fashioned doctrines of John Wesleyan Methodism into my heart and mind that will never be erased in this world or the world to come. Brother and Sister Hughes impressed me in several ways that have stayed with me during the last fifteen years. First of all, his intense devotion and loyalty to the doctrine of entire sanctification. He had a way of putting this doctrine into a man's head and heart that it stayed. Then also, he not only put the doctrine into your head and heart, but he set you afire with holy enthusiasm.

I have seen Brother Hughes tried out in the ways that try all there is in good men, and he never flinched from his devotion and sacrifice to God and Christ and the Bible. I know that it personally cost him many thousands of dollars to retain the institutions that he founded, and he personally said to me at one time ,"All I have in this world are you preachers, who are making good preaching holiness." Then I have seen Brother Hughes sacrifice for young preachers. It was one of his common expressions, when some young preacher had run out of money, for him to say, "Young man, stay and finish your education, and I will divide the last biscuit with you." This he literally and gladly did.

There is no way to express the high appreciation that I feel for Brother and Sister Hughes. Sister Hughes was a woman among women. Very few her equal, and none her superior. She died a martyr to the cause of holiness and holiness schools and no doubt millions will rise up in that great day and call her and her husband blessed, because of the influences they set going that have gone many times around the entire world. Words cannot express my personal appreciation of their high moral character, untiring sacrifice and devotion.

E. O. CHALFANT, A. B., Kingswood College, class 1912. Superintendent of Nazarene Church. Ran twenty full salvation tents all the summer.

* * * * *

AN APPRECIATION

By Rev. E. T. Franklin, A. M., President of Union College, Barbourville, Ky. Class 1903.

My first impression of "Brother Hughes," as every one called him, when I entered Asbury College in 1900, was that he was tremendously interested in the education of every young man or woman who had ambition enough to leave home for college. President Hughes was fatherly and sympathetic even in the smallest details of social or economic problems that confronted any student. Most of us were wholly unacquainted with the routine of registration, but his buoyant spirit of overwhelming enthusiasm and confidence in properly educated youth made us feel that we were in the care of a great fatherly friend.

The brief space allotted here will permit expression of only a few things among the many that might well receive notice. I have chosen three things from my observations and long acquaintance with this heroic Christian man. He was a man of conviction, he was a man of courage, and he was unselfish.

President Hughes is one of those men who have felt called to a definite work. He knew his task from the time he felt the call. It meant a rather radical departure from the usual procedure in Christian schools. He felt called to be a promoter of the doctrine and experience of holiness as taught by John Wesley and early Methodists. There was never any doubt in his mind as to the reality and extreme importance of this experience. It was not a fad with him. He believed it always, professed its power, and never lost an opportunity to propagate it.

The church has probably no more courageous spirit than that of John Wesley Hughes. He fought for the cause he loved and paid almost every possible price for his convictions. He never wavered one iota in his position because of persecution or praise, misrepresentation or flattery, economic loss or gain, the falling away of friends or the rise of the multitude to support him; but he continued to contend for the faith regardless of circumstances. I have seen him pass through some situations that would test the bravest and best, yet he never faltered in his purpose or his hope. I sat under his chapel talks for three and a half years and had several courses with him. Though outside pressure was often enough to break the ordinary spirit his zeal never dimmed. His chapel talks were a continuous avalanche of enthusiasm and loyalty to the cause he loved. His classes in theology were pronouncements of doctrine and experience with no uncertain sound.

The life of Dr. Hughes presents some of the high peaks in genuine unselfishness. He has done enough work to make him wealthy if he had worked for himself. But he put his almost unequaled energy and all his savings into others and has not waned in his love for the cause he served, or soured on the world since he finds his strength and his earthly goods well nigh gone. I never knew an earnest boy or girl, man or woman to be turned away because he was not able to pay his tuition. With Brother Hughes the cause was greater than the sacrifice necessary in promoting it. He gave himself and all he had to his boys and girls, as he called his students, and none of us ever doubted that he meant what he spoke when he repeatedly said with all the vehemence of his soul, that he would rather see us dead than to hear of our going back on God and His Kingdom.

* * * * *

DR. JOHN WESLEY HUGHES

An appreciation by Rev. Luther B. Bridgers, D. D., First General Evangelist of M. E. Church, South.

No one who has watched the progress of the Church in its effort to face the issues of modern life can fail to recognize the recent revival of the Wesleyan Doctrine of Scriptural Holiness as a potent factor in the march of human history. Though fostered by Methodism, it was not destined to be confined to the narrow channels of denominationalism, but with the "World as its Parish" it assumed an individuality and addressed its challenge to the spiritual needs of all Christendom, and hence we found among us what has been called "The Holiness Movement."

The strong prejudice against Holiness, as such, and the persistent effort Satan has made to counterfeit the experience has been the strongest proof in its favor. Burdened with erroneous teachings, fanatical extremes and inconsistent claims, it has unfortunately suffered the most at the hands of its friends.

The subject of this appreciation, as a young Spirit-baptized preacher with a love for God and His Church, shared this conviction and realized that the test of the movement would not stop with the challenge of its EXPERIENCE, but that the final decision must find its answer in the consistent conclusions based upon the premises laid down in God's Word. No religious movement ever sustained its claims by experience alone. No experience can live unless it satisfies the rightful claims of reason. Addressing himself to this task, Dr. John Wesley Hughes founded Asbury College, the first distinctive Holiness School in the United States. The heart as well as the intellect has been developed and jealously guarded. In the course of study at Asbury College metaphysical and theological dogmas challenged the claims of experience as Dr. Hughes always guarding the stimulation of the heart and stressing the value of experience, exposed the minds of his students to the theories of science and philosophy and sent them forth with a stronger experience supported by a Christian scholarship.

As one of the humblest who sat under his marvelous teaching and imbibed his godly zeal, I offer my love and appreciation. In all the varied experiences of my ministry; at times confronted by opposition and counter claims as well as glorious opportunity, I have always found a sure foundation and a place to rest my feet as I contended for the "Faith once for all delivered to the saints," and I hold as the most satisfactory weapon of my ministry, next to the Word of God, the clear, concise and exhaustive statement of Christian Faith I learned under the teaching of Dr. J. W. Hughes. It has held me steady amid the rationalistic tendencies of the age, satisfied my doubts, repelled the enemy and is today the inspiration which calls me forth to battle. May God bless Brother Hughes, who through the hundreds of young men and women he has trained and sent forth in the world, will live and labor long after he has gone to his reward.

* * * * *

AN APPRECIATION.

God has endowed men from time immemorial with a spirit of prophecy and with a burning zeal that has enabled them to proclaim the immeasurable riches of His grace and to lead souls in prayer and faith and repentance to the foot of the cross. Isaiah was one of these prophets, Jeremiah another, Amos another, and in the New Testament times the spirit of the prophets fell upon the apostles. On down through the centuries God has put His hands upon the heads and His spirit in the hearts of great men, such as Wesley, Luther, Melancthon, Fletcher, and to these men has been given the spirit of prophecy. Asbury had it and came across to plant Methodism in the wilderness of America. We consider these men great prophets because centuries separate us from their personality and from their work. Men who live in our own day and generation are prophets in the same true sense but we do not always consider them such because they are not far removed from us.

John Wesley Hughes was truly a prophet of God. At a time when religion was at low ebb in the great bluegrass country of Kentucky, when water baptism with its doctrine of immersional regeneration was being proclaimed throughout that garden spot of the world, God put His hands upon a man who dared to even preach the doctrine of instantaneous regeneration. John Wesley Hughes, like a flame of fire, went through the country preaching that a man could be born again, that he could by faith and repentance get forgiveness of sins and become justified by faith, that by witness of the Spirit he could have the joy and satisfaction of being a son of God. He was persecuted for the preaching of these doctrines. But the Wesleyan type of religion and revival was renewed in this great bluegrass country. Revivals sprang up everywhere. Men of faith began to enter the Methodist ministry and give themselves to the cause of spreading scriptural holiness over the land.

After a successful period of prophecy with many souls answering God's call, God put it upon him to establish a school of prophets. Beginning in a small way and gathering boys and girls from the State of Kentucky and finally from the whole of the United States, he gave very close attention to their training in spiritual things as well as the things of the mind. Asbury College, founded by John Wesley Hughes, has grown to be a veritable school of the prophets. Its students have entered the ministry, the evangelistic field, the field of Christian Education, the missionary work, and are successful leaders of that spiritual type of religion that is establishing the spiritual graces of Jesus Christ among the people of the world.

Truly God has called a prophet and the prophet has lived among us and his work is carried on in the hearts of men everywhere. May his mantle fall upon his students and his converts throughout the world and bring again a new refreshing from the presence of the Lord that shall be likened unto Pentecost, or unto the Wesleyan revival, or unto the great spiritual movement that is manifest everywhere under the influences of the Missionary Centenary.

The above was written by Rev. W. G. Cram, D.D., Graduated with degree of B. S. from Asbury College, 1898, received a degree of D. D. from same college in year 1918. Office now holding is Directing Secretary of the Missionary Centenary of the Methodist Episcopal Church, South. For twenty years missionary in Korea.

* * * * *

AN APPRECIATION.

By Mrs. W. W. Hopper, Director of the School of Music, Kingswood College, September 1909 to December 1914.

During my residence at Kingswood I knew Rev. J. W. Hughes as an untiring worker for the Master's cause; truly a mighty man of God, standing fearlessly and continuously for full salvation. He wrought marvelously, despite the tremendous physical, mental and financial strain under which he labored.

Two things especially stand out in my memory of his work. First, his influence on his pupils; and second, his influence on myself in leading me into the blessing of sanctification.

It was in the chapel that he made the strongest impression on his "boys and girls," as he called them. Doubtless his talks are still ringing in their hearts and lives. Morning after morning, year after year, he stood proclaiming with the greatest emphasis a "know-so" religion. "Be saved and sanctified, and then live it." This was the very core of his heart's message. And he never failed to advise the avoidance of fanaticism. "Stay in the church and keep in the middle of the road," he said.

He preached occasionally, and on Sundays, and in the weekly "Band" meetings, one of the young men or women would speak by his appointment. They delighted to have him present, for he was an attentive listener and a strict, yet loving, critic. Often he rejoiced and praised God under the preaching of the most unlearned and humble boy in school. But if one failed to declare the whole truth he was as severe in warning and admonition as a prophet of old. A wonderful leader in developing the young life in Christ Jesus!

Shortly after my first year at Kingswood Bro. Hughes came to me and said, all unexpectedly: "Miss Stone, if you and Mrs.— do not get sanctified, I do not know what I shall do." Now I knew I was saved and happy in the Lord's work, and did not think myself convicted for the blessing. I told him this. But he reminded me of my position before his young people and urged me to avoid hurting the cause. "You know it is in the Bible," he said, "you believe it; then act on principle." His earnest words set me to thinking. As a result I was wonderfully sanctified.

Just off the campus there stood a gigantic chestnut tree, which Bro. Hughes regarded as a special treasure. With great limbs spreading majestically in every direction, its symetrical appearance was a delight to the eye. To me it was always a striking symbol of the stalwart character of the man who guarded it so jealously. Even as he watched over and protected the tree, so did God watch over him, protecting His servant from all dangers, and enabling the influence of his life to go out far and wide.

I thank God for the life of Bro. Hughes. I saw him tested and tried in peculiar and unnatural ways. He stood it all and has come out more than conqueror, singing "Where He Leads Me I Will Follow."

* * * * *

THE MAN FOR THE HOUR.

By Lewis Robeson Akers, M.A., D.D., President of the Asbury Alumni Association. Class of 1903.

When a great era in human progress is about to be inaugurated, somewhere in the background God has in training the supreme man. Such men are the molders of history and the race is largely dependent upon their vision, zeal, and leadership.

The St. Paul of American Methodism was Francis Asbury, Bishop of the Methodist Episcopal Church. In a marvelous way he was privileged to assist in the organization of a great spiritual empire in the new country of America. Indefatigable in labors he toiled through virgin forests, crossed swollen streams, braved hostile savages, and endured hardships that would have overwhelmed any man not built of blood and iron, and animated by a deathless purpose.

Next to "Full Salvation," which was Asbury's dominant message, was "Christian Education." He believed that the church and the school should be united in the holy bonds of wedlock, and what God had joined together man should not put asunder. Pursuing this policy, which ideal should always be maintained by a progressive and victorious church, he was able to found, among other schools,—Bethel Academy, the first institution west of the Alleghenies and the second Methodist school in America. It was located on the bluffs overlooking the Kentucky River, in the edge of the now famous "Blue Grass Section."

When through unforeseen difficulties and vicissitudes it closed its doors, it had left nevertheless scores of men who had received educational equipment, and who, with flaming hearts and true apostolic fervor, were evangels of the cross, proclaiming far and wide a gospel that would save to the uttermost.

It seemed clearly in the Providence of God that

one hundred years later, within three miles of the site of old Bethel Academy, a college should be founded bearing the name of Asbury and carrying on the same exalted purpose and lofty ideals that animated this peerless American apostle of pioneer days. Again, it is of interest to note that the man God raised up for this purpose bore the name of the founder of Methodism—John Wesley Hughes, who in a remarkable way possessed the same passionate zeal and evangelistic ardor of the early human head of our church, believing that not only is the world our parish but that the Gospel of Christ is sufficient to reach the lost, the least, and the last man of the human race. Hence, the watchwords of this school have been and do continue to be until the present day—"Full Salvation," and "World Wide Missions."

Beginning in an humble frame building of four rooms, with three teachers and eleven students, battling against almost insurmountable difficulties, this apostolic man "carried on" for God and His Kingdom until, after fifteen years, he was privileged to see a campus of fourteen and a quarter acres, a splendid brick Administration Building, a number of other structures, a faculty of fifteen, and a student body of near three hundred. Without finances, against the bitterest opposition, misunderstood and maligned, yet firm in the consciousness of God's favor he fought the good fight of faith and prevailed.

Feeling the burden of One-Man supervision and

responsibility to be almost too heavy to be borne, as the school grew and prospered, he turned over its management to a Board of Trustees who were pledged to continue its ideals and purposes in perpetuity.

Today under the wise and able administration of its President, the Rev. Henry Clay Morrison, D. D., the school has gone forward with tremendous strides until it has become the third largest institution of the State in enrollment, and numbers its scholars from almost every State in the Union as well as from a dozen countries across the seas.

Dr. Hughes has never for a moment lost interest in his child, and lives today near the campus, is one of its trustees, makes frequent chapel talks and enjoys the confidence and love of every one in his home town of Wilmore. He is still abundant in labors, is never happier than when he is proclaiming the unsearchable riches of Christ, or about the altar helping some penitent soul to enter into the blessed experiences of pardon or purity.

John Wesley Hughes is a man of such tremendous convictions that he left a stamp upon the minds and hearts of his students never to be erased. From his class rooms there went out a steady stream of consecrated young men and women imbued with holy ideals and with the fixed purpose that Christ when He was lifted up, would draw all unto Himself.

Today, in truth, almost "From Greenland's icy mountains to India's coral strands" a host of his students are in the first line trenches of this glorious Christian warfare and are faithfully, without compromise and without a negative note, declaring that there is none other name under Heaven whereby men may be saved, save in the name of Christ; and indirectly in that day of great rewards, thousands of men of all races, creeds, and tongues will call "Blessed" the name of Asbury College and its founder, because of whom they are privileged to see the light.

Those of us who have listened to his chapel talks shall never forget their freshness and versatility. Back of the messages was the dynamic personality, and his chain of thoughts, fused through a clear thinking brain and a white hot heart, became to us "chain lightning."

Today every student, who ever sat under his ministry, feels that Brother Hughes has a vital interest in his welfare, both material and spiritual, and that to him, Asbury College was, and ever will be, a big family in Christ.

His has been the life of service and sacrifice. He has ever been true to his white ideals. Of him Lowell might have written in these words so fine:

"When I was a beggarly boy, and lived in a cellar damp,
I had not a friend nor a toy, but I had an Aladdin's lamp.
When I could not sleep for the cold, I had fire, enough in my brain,
And builded with roofs of gold, my beautiful castles in Spain."

Only the fire was in his heart as well as mind, and the beautiful castle was that of Christian character which would grace and adorn the heavenly heights. If I read aright his heart, it is his dream for this Christian school, Asbury College, to be like the great church in whose ranks he has so faithfully labored, lo, these many years—

"Unshaken as eternal hills, immovable she stands,
A mountain that shall fill the earth, a house not made with hands."

* * * * *

REV. JOHN WESLEY HUGHES, D. D.

An appreciation by Rev. Wm. S. Maxwell, B. A.

In the fall of 1895, after I had decided to answer the call to preach, which call I had felt on me from boyhood, on my way to Kentucky Wesleyan College to arrange to enter that institution in the coming January, a friend said to me, "Why don't you stop and meet John W. Hughes and see Asbury College? I think you will find there what you are looking for." Up to this time I had no recollection of ever hearing of Asbury College or Dr. Hughes.

So I stopped off at the little station of Wilmore, Ky. I walked up toward the college, which was about all there was of the town at that time. I paused at the entrance of the campus to take in the situation. I was debating in my mind whether to go on or to go back to the station and wait for a train to take me out of the little town, when I saw a man coming out of one of the buildings,—a man of medium height, slender, wearing a full beard and a Prince Albert coat. He was walking like he was going after something. On coming closer to me I noticed his beard was not groomed to indicate that he was French, German or English, just American. His salutation was "Hello, young man, where are you from?" My story was quickly given; and he turned as abruptly as he had met me and said, "I want you to meet Mamma." He turned and walked as rapidly toward the building as he had in coming from it. I asked myself the question, "Who is he and what is his position here?" The door opened and we entered and my pilot said, "Mamma this is Bro. Maxwell, you tell him about the school." His exit was as hurried as the rest of his performance had been.

I found myself in the presence of a very quiet and modest woman, slender and of medium height, a brunette, modestly but neatly dressed; the very antipode of the man who had brought me in. After a short conversation about the school, I was left alone for some reason, and I had another chance to reflect. Time and purpose do not permit me to give you my reflections. Presently Sister Hughes, whom I had learned was "mamma," came in and Bro. Hughes returned also. He addressed me thus, "Well boy, what do you think of us by now?" Without waiting for my reply said, "You can get rooms across the road." His action and decision was, "Of course you have come to stay."

This man was different from any one I had yet met. His quick action and hasty decision, in my case, was amusing and catchy. There was nothing cold or stiff in the meeting of him or his wife. He acted as if we had known each other always. Well, he had me and I was his; he won. I took the rooms and moved in to be one of his boys. I matriculated in January, 1896, for school work, and was there until the summer of 1899. But I had already, out on the roadside, matriculated in the school of friendship with him for life. From this day on, the bond of friendship between us grew. A full quarter of a century has given me ample occasion to know the man better who came so suddenly into my life on that autumn day. Not like a meteor to flash across my path and to daze me with its brightness and to leave me standing bewildered in its wake. But his coming has been more like that of a traveler coming out of the desert into a well-watered valley, an experience never to be forgotten. During my school days there sprang up a friendship different from that usually found between teacher and student. After the school at Wilmore changed hands and he started Kingswood College, I was frequently with him. He sometimes had me to conduct revivals in the school and to hold his camp meetings.

When financial trouble came, along with other troubles, he called me as a personal friend and counselor. When death came and called Mother Hughes —for such she was to all the students,—to her eternal home, I went with him to their sacred Machpelah, to bury his dead. After the funeral he accompanied me to our home, at La Grange, to spend a few days to rest his tired head and broken heart, to think the future over, and to nerve himself for the remainder of the race of life. Later in life, after he had regained his health and his shattered nerves had become normal and he was finding himself back in the battle of life, with the same old zest and zeal of former years; he found a woman of beautiful Christian character, and one who could make him a real companion and could help him in his work, in the person of Mrs. Sadie Smith Petty, and in my own home, had me make them man and wife.

These things I appreciate more than the Bachelor of Arts which he conferred on me. Scholastic degrees may mean something and they may not; it depends on the one receiving them; but real friendship is a bond stronger than death and more lasting than time.

The frank, open manner of this man of God that won me to him and has made me admire him through the years, is the thing that has repelled some. That restless nature is but the outward expression of a big soul seeking room to express itself. The lion is too large for the cage. The dynamo is too high a voltage for the lamps. The man, like his Master, has provoked a variety of opinions.

His writing has not been that of books. He has been content to write in "Human Hearts" his deeds of love and kindness. His books of theology are not to be found on shelves covered with dust, but today they girdle the globe in real men, preaching a gospel of a Christ that is able to save "From all sin."

When the records are made up, in my judgment, but a few men will have touched more lives and a greater area of the world, than John W. Hughes. No man ever sat in his theology class, for any length of time, that did not feel the fires burning in his soul, and like Isaiah, said, "Here am I; send me."

He is not negative in anything. You always know, and know at once, which side of a question he is on. He is an Andrew Jackson, without the cotton bales. He fights at close range. Fear is a word unknown to him. Defeat, if he has ever met it, he has not recognized its personality. He has the rare gift of being at home in any company. He converses easily and profitably on most subjects and makes you feel easy in his presence.

He is big enough to *give advice* and he is *Christian enough* to *take advice*. Compliments and criticism have been alike to him; they drive him to the side of the great "Rock of Ages" where he delights to live. I have heard him say under such occasions, "O, Jesus help me to be worthy."

He knows God and has been a chosen shaft in the hands of the Holy Spirit to do the work of a real Ambassador. He never drew his bow at venture; he always had an aim and a purpose. He has never willingly and purposely sacrificed friends, truth or principle. Many men complain for want of liberty who thrust their feet in Satan's fetters. They lay their heresy at the door of the sanctuary, and call their diabolical seductions evangelical revelations. Not so with this hero of Methodism. No son of Wesley has been truer to the great Bible doctrines, than this his namesake. He has both known and loved the doctrines of his church. His preaching and teaching have always been clear on the doctrines of Justification by Faith, Regeneration and the Witness of the Spirit, and Entire Sanctification subsequent to Regeneration.

* * * * *

AS I KNOW HIM.

By E. T. Adams, D. D., General Evangelist, M. E. Church, South.

I count it a high privilege to add these lines in appreciation of my friend and brother, Dr. J. W. Hughes.

Having been reared and educated outside of the holiness ranks and movement, and outside of the State of Kentucky, I never came in touch with this very remarkable and unusual character, who is author of this splendid volume, until about seven years ago. Up to this time his name was only a passing memory when referred to by some friend in connection with Kingswood College, Kentucky.

It was in the year of 1914, when Dr. Hughes was failing in health and when his noble wife, who had fought so bravely life's battles with him, was on her last bed of illness, that he and some of his friends wrote me to come to his assistance in Kingswood College. This was the closing year of his Presidency and connection with that institution. After much thought and prayer, at his urgent request, I came to see him in August of 1914, and after viewing his situation and thoroughly going over all the ground of his work, I decided to come to his assistance as a teacher, helper, friend and brother. He opened his home and heart to me and to my family, and from that hour to this I have never, for one moment, doubted his sincerity, friendship and brotherly love for me and mine.

I touched his life at its darkest hour, when his school was struggling, his health failing, his wife dying (we laid her to rest at the Christmas time) and other troubles which only God and his closest friends knew anything about. His tunnel was a long and dark one, and it seemed for a time that both mind and body would wreck; but in it all his faith never wavered. He prayed and wept through, and said, "Glory be to God, there is light ahead."

In this dark period I and some close friends advised him to go to Florida and stay until his body, mind and spirit found rest. He did so, leaving all his college problems and work on my shoulders; but I saw God was there in his school, and that He wonderfully undertook for us and gave us one of the best closings, said Dr. Hughes, he had ever had. The commencement was wonderful, really indescribable. After many years of experience in some of the best colleges and universities in the land, I have never witnessed such a program of excellence and spiritual power. It was like a holiness camp meeting at high tide. God was putting His seal on Brother Hughes' labors and making this the crowning time, when He should release him from his burdens, which He did, and brought him out of the long black tunnel into the marvelous light of freedom and peace with a shout of victory. Although it was a loss financially, it was great gain spiritually, and he could say with Job of old, "When He's tested, when He's tried me, I shall come forth as gold."

I had never met a man like Dr. Hughes. No one else ever did. There is only one J. W. Hughes. He was made on a last by himself, and they lost the pattern. He was as quick and active, at sixty, as a child, impulsive, radical, often fiery (not mad), and yet tender as a baby. He preached in the pulpit and taught in the classroom with all the energy, voice and powers he could command, like he was ready to give every ounce of his blood for the cause and subject he was presenting. If he believed a thing was true and right, he was ready to stamp a hole through the earth and bore one through the blue and die for it; and he was as strongly against it if he believed it wrong. He had not only such convictions himself, but was able to make his students and hearers feel the same.

Life to him was a real battle all the time, not to be fought by tin soldiers with toy guns and pistols, or by little dudes with red neckties and starched pants, with more collar than culture, but to be fought by real soldiers of the Pauline type, ready to suffer imprisonments, stonings, hardships, death and to die a victor. He has no patience with the "Cants" and drones. For him "to be living was sublime."

He is a man of many splendid parts; he is genial, approachable, brotherly, tender, but also stern and bold. He was often moved to great ecstacy and joy, and often sobbed with deepest emotion. He was a happy conversationalist, and no one ever spent a dull moment in his presence. He was a strong and quick thinker; met the issues squarely and made his opponents do likewise. His tremendous faith in God and in humanity at its best made him optimistic. He believed God could *take a man at his worst and put him at his best.*

He is a great theologian, and a fine metaphysician, but his creed was simple: "Salvation for all men from all sin through the blood of Jesus," and "Holiness without which no man can see God." His pet themes were, *"A Horrible Hell"* for the wicked and a *"Beautiful Heaven"* for the holy. His spirit, his faith and creed took hold of you. He is one of the greatest religious and doctrinal teachers of his time. He made character of the solid, rugged type, not little sentimental "sissies," but men and women who knew and believed something and who were ready to die for it. His students have circled the globe and have become moral and religious leaders of their time and clime. He is a strong and forceful preacher, and one of the greatest soul winners of his day. As an Evangelist, it was often said of him, "He either had a revival or a riot," and often both, when he conducted a meeting. He is one of the strongest advocates and teachers of Bible holiness since the days of John Wesley and Adam Clarke.

But time would fail me to write all I know and feel in my heart of appreciation of this great and white soul. He is my friend and neighbor, and has been like a father to my family. He has meant more to me than he knows, and more than I can tell. I always count it a high privilege and pleasure to be in his presence. No life ever touched him who was not better for the touch. Earth will be poorer, my heart will be sadder, but Heaven will be richer when he goes hence.

* * * * *

AN APPRECIATION.

Rev. Chas. H. Neal, B. A. Class of 1899.

The Lord said upon one occasion:

"Hast thou considered my servant Job, that there is none like him in the earth?"

The same might be said of J. W. Hughes. There was never anyone who looked like him or who could act like him. His personal appearance such that he would be noticed in any crowd and possessing a voice and personality certain to gain attention whenever and wherever he arose to address an audience—even where others had "put them to sleep"—to those who knew him best the above statement will not seem unreasonable.

I shall speak of him as in the past, not because I feel that his life and labors have ended, but the tragedy of advancing years and separated interests makes it highly probable that never in this world will we again enjoy those intimate associations of the past. He was, and is, my friend as only God knows what a true friend can be, but I can only look at him now as afar off and feel that in other days I failed to enjoy and profit by his friendship and counsel as I might have, though both have had much to do with whatever good there may be in me.

My knowledge of him goes back into the past when I, a freckled-faced, barefoot, green country boy, first saw him, a long lanky young circuit rider at my old home in the hills of Kentucky. From that time until now I have never lost sight of him or he of me, though for years at a time we have not met.

For four and a half years it was my privilege to be with him in Asbury College. I say with him instead of under him, as it would be proper to say, because he had that way about him, which, while never losing his sense of authority nor allowing you to lose sight of it, nevertheless his free, confidential and jovial manner always put the most timid at ease.

I graduated from Asbury College with the Bachelor of Arts degree in 1899. Looking back now over those years of intimate associations and personal contact I can see those elements of greatness which in my youth and ignorance I could not then fully appreciate. He was one of those rare characters whose worth can only be seen when the cobwebs of familiarity, prejudices, jealousy and misunderstandings have been swept away by the hand of time and our hearts tempered by sorrows, regrets and the consciousness of our own shortcomings.

Possessing twice the energy his physical make-up would indicate, he could undergo more of the telling trials and labors of life than any man it has been my privilege to know. As a preacher he had no equal because nobody preached like him. The same zeal and uniqueness of manner he carried into the class room. I have seen him face disaster with a courage and calmness worthy of a great general on the battlefield. Religion was his passion, theme and practice of life, yet he never lost his balance in orthodox theology. Though sometimes criticised by the church to which he gave his life he nevertheless remained true and loyal to the doctrines and polity of Methodism. He has not thus far been acclaimed great as greatness goes, because he has raised such a cloud of dust that the world has not been able to see him. That cloud of dust has begun to settle upon the world in the form of men and women making good as a result of his labors, sacrifices and soul agony. Some day we may see and understand.

Though the care-free days of youth have gone, the experiences of mature years have filled my mind with a thousand things, men and women have come into my life and gone and the stretch of years made furrows upon my brow, yet it seems as but yesterday when I heard the ring of his voice in praise and song and exhortation. His form, though to men's eyes not comely, stands out before me like a guide post pointing me onward and upward; his voice calls to me out of the fog as a buoy bell to a bewildered sailor of the sea; his friendship comes to me over the years with the fragrance of springtime flowers. He taught me to be a man, to love men, to respect men, but to fear only God.

I know not what others have said about him in the book of his life that is now being written. It matters not. To me he stands out above the multitudes as my true and tried friend. I shall never see his like again. When the time comes for him to go he can unbuckle the sword and lay it down with the feeling that he gave his best. He has given the world his message in language they could understand. The world has known where he stood. He has not been afraid to live and I think he will not be afraid to die.

* * * * *

AN APPRECIATION.

Of Rev. John Wesley Hughes, D. D. by Rev. W. L. Clark, D. D. B. A. Class of 1895.

It is a very common thing for us to speak words of commendation and praise of our relatives, neighbors, friends, and countrymen, when they have departed this life, when it is too late to help them by any words of praise we might speak, or deeds of kindness we might show: so contrary to this common blunder, I find pleasure in writing a few lines of appreciation of Rev. J. W. Hughes, my benefactor, teacher, fellow townsman and personal friend.

To those who have known Dr. Hughes when he was in his prime and giving his all to the promotion of Christian Education in general and to Asbury College in particular, it is hardly necessary to say that without stint or reservation he gave himself whole heartedly to whatever he did, that the scripture which says, "Whatsoever thy hand findeth to do, do with all your might," could very fittingly be applied to John Wesley Hughes. If it was the raising of money to educate a poor boy, teaching a class in thology, debating with his antagonist, meeting a train, listening to a lecture, preaching a sermon, or talking to a sinner about his soul, if Dr. Hughes was that man it was done with all his might. He did not then, and does not now, know how to do things by halves. Whatsoever he does, he does with all his might. Thus his enemies and those who did not agree with him on religious and theological questions were forced at least to admire and appreciate his frankness and honesty.

It is a well known fact that Dr. Hughes has been a great soul winner, and if I should be called upon to answer, "What is the secret of his success?" I should answer. 1. He knew God as his personal Savior and sanctifier. 2. He positively testified to this under all circumstances. The world and the church has ever been willing to listen to a man who knows, and knows that he knows something, and is so positive about it that he is not afraid to let men or devils know what he believes and stands for.

Dr. Hughes, like Paul, could and would say, "For I know whom I have believed, and am persuaded that he is able to keep that which I have committed unto him against that day." He was ever willing to give a reason for the hope that was in him, and to give it to all men.

Dr. Hughes and the Holiness Movement.—For more than thirty years what is known as the modern holiness movement (which was nothing more or less than a reviving of the old Wesleyan doctrine of spreading scriptural holiness over the land) came into the church in general and into the Methodist church in particular, Dr. Hughes having entered into this experience when a young man, and minister, with his evangelistic qualities and dogmatic positiveness, soon became one of the prominent figures in the effort to restore to the church in general, apostolic Christianity, and to bring the Methodist church, in particular, back to her original mission, according to Mr. Wesley, "Spreading scriptural holiness over these lands:" Just so Dr. Hughes, in 1890, in response to a divine impression, and visible human need, started Asbury College, in Wilmore, Ky. Thus he founded, promoted, sacrificed for, and acted as the President for fifteen years, of this child of Providence—that which stands as one of the greatest accomplishments in this age, and will doubtless through all eternity prove to be his greatest joy and source of reward. If he had done nothing else than start, run, and foster Asbury College, as its sole owner, he would have thereby accomplished more for Bible Christianity than the average man in the whole of his life. For his pupils have gone out to become a success as authors, teachers, doctors, lawyers and preachers, rising even to the highest position of honor in the church of God.

Dr. Hughes, being a very positive man, left his impress upon his converts and pupils. When he was in his prime, evangelistic fires were kindled almost everywhere he went. His converts were positive in the assertion of their Christian faith. The same can be said of his pupils. Those who went through Asbury College while J. W. Hughes was President, received in class room, on the platform, and in private contact with him, such an influence as to make a lasting impression. They went out with such absolute certainty in their utterances that it bordered on dogmatic utterance and everywhere you could hear it said, "You must be one of John Hughes' converts, or you must have been to Asbury College." But this is no mean compliment; Napoleon possessed it, Stonewall Jackson had it, and Theodore Roosevelt illustrated it. The facts are that every man in church or state, or moral reform, who counts for his cause must have a positiveness, an aggressiveness that dares, and does, or this generation will pass him by as one that is not worth while.

My first knowledge of Dr. Hughes was as a pastor. He was assigned by the Kentucky Conference to the Campbellsburg Circuit, in the bounds of which I lived as a country boy. He, with his good wife, had such enthusiasm, such zeal, such constant singing and praying in the homes of the people, and up and down the road side, that the whole community was stirred. It was said that "They that turn the world upside down had come hither also." Some said he was beside himself, others praised him, and still others received the gospel he preached and were saved by the Christ he loved and served. Among those blessed during these earlier years of his successful ministry, was Miss Loulie M. Stratton, a country school teacher, and afterward for a number of years a teacher in Asbury College. Another was Rev. W. F. Wyatt, now for many years a successful member of the Kentucky Conference. It was through the influence of these two, more than any other human instrumentality, that I myself, came to know Jesus Christ, so that I count myself his spiritual grandson. In after years, it was my privilege to sit in his class room, so I congratulate myself for the benefits received from his indomitable will, his dogmatic tenacity, his religious constancy with which he moved among those his life touched.

Dr. Hughes, like many other honorable and great men, and like his Lord, was born of poor parents, no disgrace, but often very inconvenient. As a result, he experienced the struggles common to an ambitious youth to procure an education, but this he did, first in Kentucky Wesleyan College and then in Vanderbilt University. The sacrifice and economy he had to practice here helped to prepare him for whatever sacrifice would be necessary when he entered the ministry as a member of the Kentucky Conference. And he located after thirteen years of successful pastorate to evangelize, and then to start Asbury College. He was well trained for the necessary economy that he was afterwards called upon to exercise in order to make Asbury College a success. When he started Asbury College in 1890 he had only saved about $5,000, but from this small beginning, by energy, and rigid economy, and some little assistance from friends, he had built an institution in fifteen years that was worth $40,000—which he turned over to the holiness people for $25,000, and which institution today is worth more than a half million dollars, and stands as a living monument to the praise of its founder and promoters, among whom there has been no greater than the Rev. H. C. Morrison, D. D., its present president.

Possibly the strongest test of a man's real worth, and contribution to the world is the fruit of his labor placed upon the markets of the world's competition. Here our brother shines with the stars of the first magnitude.

Dr. Hughes now lives in the city of Wilmore, Ky., and is still active in church duties and pulpit utterances. As his pastor at present, I can truthfully say, "He is one of the best boosters in an audience I ever saw." A man can hardly say a good thing if he is in the audience, that he does not respond with a hearty, "Amen." May his bow abide in strength many years yet to bless the church with his life and ministry.

* * * * *

AN APPRECIATION.

Rev. W. D. Akers, A. B. D. D.

In 1901, Rev. J. W. Hughes invited me to become a member of the faculty of Asbury College, Wilmore, Ky. For three years I was associated with him in the most delightful, and, I believe, most profitable work of my life. I shall always regard it as a high honor, and a great privilege, to have known Asbury in her earlier days, and to have brone some humble part in helping a goodly number of her students to enter upon lives of usefulness, and, in some cases, into lives of conspicuous service for God and man. This institution was conceived in the spirit of devotion to the interests of the kingdom of God, and brought forth through prayer.

When Brother and Sister Hughes began their humble work in a then obscure hamlet in Kentucky, the warmest friend of the enterprise did not dare dream of the Asbury of today, with its splendid buildings, and, in every way, enlarged facilities for carrying out the cherished desire of its founders to make it a great soul-saving institution, and a recruiting station where young men and women could be equipped intellectually and spiritually for real service for God in the pastoral, evangelistic and mission fields of the world. Asbury needs to make no apology for the work done in the days of her infancy. Her former students in all lands are testifying to what she did for them while within her walls. Though her facilities for doing college work were limited, she did honest, conscientious work.

Brother and Sister Hughes made a deep impress upon the student body. They had a consuming passion for souls, and imparted that passion to the young people under their care. Brother Hughes had an unusual ability in driving the truth home, and in imparting the evangelistic spirit to those who went out from the college to do service for the Master, as a host of earnest workers at home and abroad will testify. His earnestness in the class room, as well as outside of it, was contagious.

The Asbury spirit is a notable phenomenon in the religious world. Brother and Sister Hughes literally poured out their lives for others. The sainted Mary Wallingford Hughes was a mother to the entire Asbury family, and a multitude will rise up in the great day to call her blessed. Her beautiful, unselfish life was a benediction to all with whom she came in contact. Of her it may be truly said: "She hath done what she could."

The writer will never forget Brother Hughes' chapel talks. They were models of fresh, lucid, fervent, practical speech. Their educational and inspirational value to the student body was incalculable. That the new Asbury may maintain the old spirit, and never lose her *uniqueness* among the colleges of the land, is our prayer.

While the old motto, "Industry, Thoroughness, Salvation," has disappeared from sight with the dismantled walls of her old "Administration Building," it still flames out in the burning zeal, culture, conscientiousness and consecration of her sons and daughters. While time shall last Brother and Sister Hughes will continue to multiply themselves in the fruitful lives of those who have gone out of Asbury, and in the lives of those who shall yet go out to bless the world. They can each truly say, in the language of the Latin poet: "Exegi monmentun acre perennius; I have erected a monument more lasting than brass." When we contrast the little frame building in which they began their humble work, with the group of magnificient buildings which now adorn the campus; the faculty of only four members and the student body of only eleven persons, with the present large faculty and six hundred students, we may well exclaim, "What hath God wrought!"

Turning our eyes toward the future, we see in vision, an ever enlarging institution. We see building added to building; constantly enlarging facilities for imparting knowledge; an increasing number of young people crowding its halls, then going out to the ends of the earth to bear the tidings of full salvation to a lost world. In my vision, I see a great multitude standing upon the glassy sea, before the throne of God, clothed in white robes, with

APPRECIATIONS

the emblems of victory in their hands, and with harp and voice giving praise "to the Lamb who was slain." In that number I see Brother and Sister Hughes, with radiant faces, surrounded by former Asbury students and others conducted to glory by them.

May the institution founded amid their prayers and tears become more and more a blessing to this sin-sick world. A better place at which to kindle the fires of our devotion, around which to center our prayers, and to which we may give our help, in every way, does not exist in this world.

After Bro. Hughes' successful administration, it was a most fortunate thing for Asbury, that some years ago, Dr. H. C. Morrison was chosen as its president. Under his wise leadership, its growth has been phenomenal. May he be spared many years to lead it to greater heights of prosperity and power.

* * * * *

AN APPRECIATION.

It has been my good fortune and great pleasure to know intimately, for a number of years, Dr. J. W. Hughes, and both of his excellent wives.

Having been associated with him in educational work for about a dozen years, at Wilmore and Kingswood, Kentucky, I can speak with perfect assurance concerning his ability as a college president: it was wonderful—far above the recognition of most who praised him. After close connection with a dozen institutions of higher learning, I can truthfully declare Dr. Hughes unexcelled by any president or chancellor under whom it has been my privilege to study or to serve.

"Brother Hughes" (as I best like to call him) possesses keen insight, unusual tact, good judgment, old-fashioned common-sense, *rare* appreciation, uncommon kindness of heart, genuine sympathy, undying devotion to principle, loyalty to friends, the "lost-art" of friendship, real vision, high ideals, "personal magnetism," and an exemplary character. He puts prayer, power, and persistence into every work. Sacrifice has been the meat of his service. He knows how to forgive enemies, to practice humility, to do with his might whatsoever his hands find to do, to put *himself* into his labors; to trust, and wait, and hope—and in all things to give thanks with cheerfulness.

It is the misfortune of the truly great, to project themselves *away* from their comrades, and, lonely, await their meed of praise from the lips of the unborn.

So the man and his work cannot be weighed by us. But we who know and appreciate him most, can glimpse the future fame. And to measure *him* is but to begin: he lives in the lives and aspirations of hundreds whom he finely fitted and fully fixed in successful service.

May God *continue* his life and labors among us!

With warmest appreciation,

THEDA COBLEIGH PEAKE, M. A., Prof. Olivet University, Ill.

AN APPRECIATION.

By Prof. M. L. Smith, A. M., Class of 1915. M. A. and B. D., Emory University.

In June 1910, Dr. Beverly Carradine, that genius of American pulpits, came to my home town, Lanett, Alabama ,for a ten-days' revival meeting. At this time a young preacher, I was very ambitious for a college education. Very few men have shown greater interest in the education of young men and women than Dr Carradine. It is said of him that during his ministry he gave financial help to between thirty and forty such young people. He insisted on my going to Kingswood College, Kentucky, which had been founded in 1906 by his life-long friend, Dr. J. W. Hughes, who was at that time its president.

In September I entered the freshman class at Kingswood. For that year about two hundred students (a delightful size student body) enrolled in all departments. During my residence of five years about a thousand young men and women came and went, but no one ever entered who was not soon personally known by Dr. Hughes and who could not have shared his last penny if necessary to complete his or her education. These are the things that have made his college career eminently successful, for not only did the students acquaint themselves with the sciences, mathematics, languages and theology, but they caught something of his spirit of unselfishness, sympathy and passion for a needy world. And the world—not America only, but China, Japan, India, Korea, Africa etc.—has felt the power of this spirit as it laid its hand upon his boys and girls who are scattered on every continent of the earth, and I fully believe that out of the devotion and self-sacrifice of Dr. J. W. Hughes a new day has come to the world.

In 1913 I received the B. A. degree, and the following years I taught as an associate in the Department of Ancient Languages. During these two years I also took post-graduate work looking forward to the M. A. degree which was awarded me in 1915. During these two years, having been a member of the faculty, I was led into a more intimate acquaintance with the president, for in the business relationships, as well as in other phases of life, the real test comes. Dr. Hughes in this capacity had the confidence and admiration of all those who were associated with him.

In 1915, after twenty-five years of successful college work, Dr. Hughes gave up the psesidency of Kingswood College in order to carry out the urgent requests of his many friends, namely, to write the story of his life and to put into written form the results of his life-long study along theolgical and philosophical lines. This literary work, which is needed is going to add much to a clearer understanding of the field of Biblical study. I bespeak for these volumes a wide circulation and hope that every young preacher especially, shall have them in his library.

This decision, however, on the part of Dr. Hughes

to discontinue his college work probably affected my whole life, for it was he who had been the friend and counsellor of every young man and woman in Kingswood College, who had influenced the continuation of my education, an influence for which I shall forever be grateful. In December of 1917, therefore, I entered Emory University and continued my work until August 1921, at which time I received the M. A. and B. D. degrees.

The reader now sees how vitally my life has been touched by the influence of Dr. Hughes. In just this way he touched the lives of all that came under his lufluence, and, as I have already said, this was not done alone through the courses offered at Kingswood College, but by a life lived at its best.

* * * * *

AN APPRECIATION

Of Dr. J. W. Hughes, by Rev. F. B. Jones, Presiding Elder, Kentucky Conference.

I have known Brother Hughes from my early childhood. We were born and reared in the same county. When I was yet a lad he frequently visited my father's house. I remember him at that time as a tall, straight, vigorous young man full of life and zeal for his Master. He was respected by all who knew him for his devout spirit and determined purpose to follow his Lord despite the many difficulties which confronted him. Early in life our paths diverged and I saw him less frequently until later years.

During my second year at Kentucky Wesleyan College, Winchester, Kentucky, Brother Hughes founded Asbury College at Wilmore, Kentucky. In 1891 I matriculated in this school where I found my friend at the head of this young but growing institution. He had lost none of his faith, zeal or courage, but with more difficulties than he had ever encountered before, was pushing ahead, feeling sure that God had called him to this great work and believed with confidence that God, who had called, would see him through

To start an independent Holiness school with little money and few sympathizers at the time Asbury was founded, required more grit and grace than the average man possessed. To stick to this task through losses, crosses and persecutions—which I chanced to know came to the leader of this institution—required indomitable will and undaunted faith in God.

In the early days of Asbury, Brother Hughes was President, Business Manager, Financial Agent, and Teacher of Theology. Having been a close student of the Bible and sometime student in Vanderbilt University, he was thoroughly conversant with the fundamental doctrines of the Bible and Theology and knew how to drill them into the minds and lives of those under his care in such a way that they never could be erased. I do not know of a young man that sat under Brother Hughes that ever became a skeptic or destructive critic.

Hundreds who have gone out from Asbury stand

APPRECIATIONS

firm today for the principles for which she was founded, and through her religious influence and mental training are able to stand well with their fellows in every walk of life. Many missionaries, teachers, evangelists, pastors, and presiding elders (and at least one bishop) who, have been trained at Asbury, are helping to redeem the world. Her missionaries have girdled the globe, until it can be truthfully said the sun never sets on her missionaries.

From the beginning, Brother Hughes held to the highest ideals of Christian education, believing that the training of the soul was of even more importance than that of the mind, although the mind was never neglected. Because of these high ideals of spiritual needs, but few persons have ever gone through this institution that have not been brought into a knowledge of the saving grace of our Lord, and many have entered into the fullness of His sanctifying grace.

I doubt that any man has ever accomplished more for good under so many difficulties than has this man of God, by the founding of Asbury College, and thus making it possible to do the work that has been done here. Brother Hughes, like many another who has wrought well, will not be appreciated fully by the world until he has been in Heaven long enough to enjoy much of the fruits of his toil.

I chanced to be the second graduate of Asbury College, having taken my A. B. degree from this institution on May 27, 1894.

AN APPRECIATION

From Rev. Henry W. Bromley, M. A. D. D., Class of 1901.

It was the vision, conviction, enthusiasm, and unconquerable courage of the Reverend John Wesley Hughes that brought about my conversion to Christ and entrance to the ministry. His call of God to found a school which would cultivate the heart as well as the head, has meant a like experience to hundreds of other men, who, in evangelistic field and pastoral pulpit, in professional chair, and mission land, are winning hundreds of thousands to Christ.

The salvation of men was the burning passion of Dr. Hughes' life, and he had in a superlative degree, the ability to transmit his enthusiasm to his students. I have never heard his chapel talks surpassed in warmth, diversity, and interest of material. He was variety itself. Students felt that to miss them was a personal loss. And he never had the *slightest jealousy* of *other capable men*, whom he *delighted to bring to his platform*. He was never happy till the greatest possible effort had been made to save the last sinner in school. What wonderful spiritual times we had during those struggling days of Asbury College! And though the school was limited in equipment and other resources, its graduates have ranked with those of the best schools of the Church.

I have never known a more liberal-hearted soul than Dr. Hughes. He veritably educated hundreds at his own expense. The humblest and most needy student always had access to his heart.

Whatever he attempted to teach he could indelibly impress upon his students. I shall never forget *Ralston's Elements of Divinity, Butler's Analogy,* and *Hamilton's Metaphysics.* My lecture work along philosophical and theological lines today, has its genesis in Dr. Hughes' class room. He made a chap feel like making something out of himself. And into those who had the soil to take it, he planted religious truth, from which they will never get away.

He is an enjoyable traveling companion. He, my brother Charles, and myself took a trip together to Palestine—and what variety he put into that journey!

Some men have differed with Dr. Hughes as to his views, and some as to his methods, but none who have known him intimately, as I have known him, have doubted his sincerity, fidelity to conviction, and unbounded earnestness in the propagation of his beliefs.

I do not believe in waiting till men are dead to do them honor. The sensible time to express regard is while they are living.

* * * * *

AN APPRECIATION

By Lena Hayes Tucker, A. B., A. M., Kingswood College, and some time teacher.

As we recall the names of great men who have lived and wrought in Breckenridge County, none is more inspiring than that of Rev. J. W. Hughes, the founder of Asbury and Kingswood Colleges. He had a great vision and followed its gleam.

Dr. Hughes was a teacher of the highest type, clear and simple in his illustrations and applications to every day life. He was a preacher of rare ability, convincing in argument, with a comprehensive knowledge of the Holy Scriptures, and he taught clearly the fundamental truths of the Bible and Theology. At the call of God to found a second Holiness College, Brother Hughes, after casting about for some time, bought a farm of one thousand acres, in Breckenridge County, sixty-five miles Southwest of Louisville, Kentucky—an ideal retreat for student life.

When he announced his purpose, it seemed to any other than the man of strong faith an impossible undertaking, and the entire country stood amazed at the project. But with undaunted courage, untiring energy, and faith in God, this hero of faith called about him workmen to fell the trees of the forest, architects, stone masons and carpenters, and plans were made for the erection of the beautiful buildings, which were put up in such a short time, it seemed almost a miracle.

Roads had to be opened up. At his own expense, the roads were put in good condition. The camp ground was cleared; a tabernacle and cottages were built, and all preparations were made for the first Holiness Camp Meeting ever held in Breckenridge County.

To his platform were brought some of the strongest preachers in this country, namely: Doctors Mc-

Laughlin, Gross Alexander, Carradine, Walker, and Fowler, Rev. Bud Robinson, and other outstanding leaders in the Holiness ranks. These great preachers were staunch friends of Brother Hughes and always gave their hearty endorsement to the work of his institution.

At these annual camp meetings, the spirit of the Lord came upon the people and great revivals of religion broke out, and many souls were genuinely saved or sanctified. As a result of these revival efforts, the whole country was blessed and refreshed, and a great spiritual and educational awakening was felt, and many of our substantial citizens sent their sons and daughters to Kingswood College, where they received an education of both head and heart.

Words are inadequate to express the gratitude of my heart for the great sacrifice our beloved president and his godly wife and faculty made to establish a Christian college in our midst. The influence of their lives and teaching lives on. While Sister Hughes has passed to her reward, her good works follow her. The dearest interest of her heart was the success of the college. Peace to her memory! She blessed and inspired every life she touched. She exerted a powerful influence over the student body for good, and led many souls into the light. How fitting the words "Except a grain of wheat fall into the earth and die, it cannot bring forth."

While the school was a great financial loss to Brother Hughes, it was a great gain to our county, as it brought greater prosperity to the surrounding country. It was an open door of opportunity to many who otherwise could not have enjoyed the blessings of a Christian education.

Brother Hughes was devoted to the upbuilding of the common people. He was bubbling over with an irrepressible enthusiasm and love for men, and considered all men his brothers.

He regarded religion, common sense, and energy as requisites for success in any life, without which any life would be a failure.

He was naturally endowed with good common sense, and a store of energy which seemed well nigh inexhaustable. He had a mind hungry for knowledge, and was a great student. Determination, moral earnestness, sincerity and self reliance were striking traits of his character. He had a great passion for righteousness and the courage of his convictions in the face of fierce opposition.

His life's work is lasting; eternity only will reveal the greatness of his work. By his generous and philanthropic spirit, many a life has been lifted to a higher plane of usefulness and inspired to attempt great things for God. He has sent out from these Holiness Colleges, a great number of faithful workers into the ministry at home and the mission fields abroad, who are carrying the gospel of full salvation into the uttermost parts of the earth. These are blessing humanity and honoring God with their consecrated lives. When these come up to the judgment from China, Korea, Africa, Japan, India and America with all the redeemed they have won for Christ, then will Brother Hughes be glad for the investment of his life in this great work.

Many are the diamonds he has picked out of the rough and polished into beauty with a Christian education. These are the light of the world today in many dark places; yea, the very salt of the earth.

In that great day when Christ comes to make up His Jewels, many will shine in glory who were brought into the light through the saving influence of Asbury and Kingswood Colleges. These hundreds and thousands of souls who have been blessed through his influence are his valuable assets, far better than gold or bank stock or any earthly treasures. How true the words of the Master, "Whosoever will lose his life for my sake, shall find it."

FINIS.

Pentecostal Publishing Company Collection

The Asbury Theological Seminary library was started in 1939 to meet the needs of a new theological institution based on the teaching of holiness and sanctification in the Wesleyan tradition. It moved to its current building in 1967, when it was named after Bergie Lee Fisher, an innovator in the new and exciting telephone business of the day, and a close friend of Asbury's founder and first president, H.C. Morrison.

The B.L. Fisher Library currently houses a collection of nearly half a million print and electronic resources to help further its educational mission to support the students, staff, and faculty of Asbury Theological Seminary. It also houses several important archival collections, including the papers of E. Stanley Jones and Hannah Whitall Smith. In addition, the library has focused on building an extensive collection of Pentecostal-Holiness, and Wesleyan material.

In its efforts to provide resources to the greater academic community, B.L. Fisher Library has developed First Fruits Press to supply electronic material freely to a global audience. In his will, Asbury's founder H.C. Morrison left his publishing company, the Pentecostal Publishing Company, to Asbury Theological Seminary. For several years, many of these rare items of the Pentecostal-Holiness tradition, have been unseen or unused by scholars in the field of Pentecostal Studies. First Fruits Press is pleased to bring these materials back to the attention of the Scholarly Community in a digital format, open and freely accessible to the world.

asburyseminary.edu
800.2ASBURY
204 North Lexington Avenue
Wilmore, Kentucky 40390

www.ingramcontent.com/pod-product-compliance
Lightning Source LLC
Chambersburg PA
CBHW051749040426
42446CB00007B/278